In God's Presence

—A Daily Devotional—

Bridgette Marie

In God's Presence

—A Daily Devotional—

Copyright © 2016 Bridgette Marie

Suggested daily scriptures used in this book recommend the following versions.

ESV, English Standard Version. The Holy Bible, English Standard Version Copyright © 2001 by Crossway Bibles, a publishing ministry of Good News Publishers.

GNT, Good News Translation. Copyright © 1992 by American Bible Society.

NIV, New International Version. Holy Bible, New International Version®, NIV® Copyright © 1973, 1978, 1984, 2011 by Biblica, Inc.

NLT, New Living Translation. Holy Bible, New Living Translation, copyright ©1996, 2004, 2007 by Tyndale House Foundation.

Dedication

I dedicate this book to my parents, Ken and Wendy. It is because of you that I am so passionate about my walk with Christ. You've taught me to love God and love people, seek Him with my whole heart and be an authentic representative of God on the earth.

To my fiancé, Jamar, it is because of you that I know God has called me to a higher calling. Thank you for pushing me to new heights and challenging me to be better as I seek God daily.

To Minister Rita, thank you for pushing me to my full potential and helping me realize that this walk with Christ is not about me.

To my big sister, Tiffani, thank you for being my angel here on earth and always encouraging me to do better.

To my 14 nieces and nephews, I pray that as you grow you will witness Gods presence daily and choose to walk in the purpose he has destined for your life.

To Candice, thank you for those late nights in the library. It's because of you that I stayed focused and motivated to complete this mandate from God.

To the ladies in my Connection Group, we are connected for life. It's because of you that I have the desire to reach souls for Gods kingdom. When I wanted to give up, I thought of you and realized that I couldn't quit.

To my "BigMama" LillieMae, I hope I'm making you proud. Your legacy lives on!

Lastly, I dedicate this to my friend Loriana "AloriJoh" Johnson, it is because of your death that I found new meaning to my writing and have really let go and allowed God to use me like only he can.

Foreword

It is with great hope that you become excited and charged in your spirit, after reading *In God's Presence.*

There is no better place to be than in the presence of God. In that place, you will find peace that surpasses your understanding, rest for your soul, comfort in the time of storm and assurance that God absolutely loves and adores you.

In God's Presence will transform your life. After reading this book you will acquire an insatiable appetite for more of God's word. Your intimacy with God will be unmeasurable and everlasting, as you saturate yourself in daily devotional reading.

The inspirations pinned in this book by Bridgette Marie, will electrify your inner man, resulting in a discourse with you and God that will be a loving dialogue of your spirit and God's Spirit. She knows firsthand what intimacy with God is like. Her daily devotion with God is the result of this book. Her prophetic gifting has been released through *In God's Presence*.

COME, LET'S ENJOY IN GOD'S PRESENCE.

—Minister Rita Williams-Steel
Co-laborer in the Gospel
Bethel Unspeakable Joy Church, Inc.

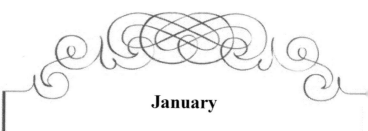

January

"You will keep in perfect peace all who trust in you, all whose thoughts are fixed on you!"

—Isaiah 26:3 (NLT)

January 1
Our Greatest Example

Luke 6 (NIV)

Jesus was the greatest example for us on the earth. He showed us how to love God and how to love people, in the flesh and also in the spirit. Be willing to follow the example that Jesus has set for us, this will help you lead others to salvation. Follow Christ's example and it will lead you to eternal life.

You may feel like you're doing everything right, yet you still don't have what your heart desires. Remember that your inheritance awaits you in the heavenly realm. God will bestow on you many great things while you walk the earth, but your greatest inheritance is in heaven.

NOTES:

January 2
The Miracle Worker

Job 11:13-19 (ESV)

God is a miracle worker! If you surrender all to him and allow him to work on your behalf, you'll see him work in miraculous ways. Prepare your heart for what God has for you. It may not be exactly how you planned it for your life, but it's an excellent plan because it comes from God.

Acknowledge that God took you from darkness and has shown you his marvelous light. Don't revert backwards, but keep pressing forward to the mark. God will hold your hand every step of the way, and he will get you to the perfect place he wants you to be. It will be a place of peace, joy and sweet rest in him.

NOTES:

January 3
Don't Give In To Temptation

Romans 12:2 (GNT)

Once you have accepted Jesus Christ as your Savior, you begin to look at things differently in the spirit and in the flesh. Knowing that things you used to do weren't like God; the things you used to say didn't represent God; the things you used to participate in were not of God. Don't be lured into what the world offers you, it will only lead to death. It is appeasing to the natural eye, but it will watch you crumble.

It is your choice whether to give in to what the world has to offer or to stand firm on the foundation that Christ built for you, through God. You may veer off track from time to time, but never take your eyes off God. He is the only one that can help you stay on track, the only one that can help you stay rooted so that you don't give into the temptations that the world offers you daily.

NOTES:

January 4
The Impossible Made Possible

John 1:1-3 (GNT)

God is our foundation! God is the Word! Nothing is made possible without him. We cannot get to God the Father, except through his son Jesus Christ. God is the mastermind behind all that you see in the flesh and all that you witness and experience in the spirit. God created everything with a purpose, knowing what benefit it would have for his kingdom.

There is nothing that can separate you from the greatness of God. Hold fast to the true fact that God is the beginning and he is the end. Nothing can happen unless God allows it to happen, nothing can take place unless God allows it to take place, and nothing will come to pass unless God allows it to come to pass. Stay true to the Word of God; his Word will never fail and it will never return to you void.

NOTES:

January 5
Adhere To The Voice of God

Job 33 (NLT)

God is always speaking. Are you listening? God will never put on you more than you can bear. In fact, everything that you go through is intended just for you—to strengthen you, to teach you, to add to your testimony, to prove to you that God is real. God controls all things, the good and the not so good. What has God been telling you lately through your circumstances?

God holds the answers to all of your questions. God will only reveal to you what he wants you to know about whatever it is you ask of him. Majority of the time he wants to see if you trust him and if you'll stand firm on his promises for your life. You'll go through many things over the course of your life. Will you allow the Holy Spirit to guide you every step of the way while you walk by faith?

NOTES:

January 6
The Test Of Faith

Job 34:3-4 (ESV)

There are many things that we encounter daily that will test our faith in God. Some things more than others are more challenging. Even when you are tested, how often do you give in? Having a relationship with Christ doesn't mean that you will not go through challenges. It means that you are equipped to deal with everything that comes your way on a daily basis.

Ask God to give you the wisdom daily to distinguish between what God has sent and what the evil one has sent. Be cautious, because some things look good and are wrapped nicely, but are not sent by God. Be a good judge of character. Choose to obtain clarity from God in the areas of your life that you are not clear about.

NOTES:

January 7
Live By Faith

2 Corinthians 5:7 (ESV)

Everything that you do in life should be by faith and not by sight. Believe in the impossible and trust that the impossible can turn into miracles when God is involved. Remembering always, that there is nothing that God can't do. Faith teaches us to trust God even when we can't see the outcome. Faith teaches us to have confidence in a higher being (God) because he holds all of the answers to our questions and the solutions to our problems.

Walking by faith means to not lean on your own understanding, which leads to destruction, but to follow the path that God laid out for you even if you can't see the outcome. God knows the end at the beginning.

NOTES:

January 8
Watch God Work

Psalm 34:17-18 (GNT)

God is always near and he hears you when you call. He will deliver you from all of your problems and walk you right to your solutions. Don't allow your circumstances to burden you. Don't allow your situations to get the best of you. God will deliver you, God will make you whole again, and God will be the one to give you increase. The moment you stop worrying about your problems will be the very moment God turns your situation around.

God doesn't work on your timing, but he does work on your behalf. So watch God work! Thank him in advance for the abundant blessings that your hands won't be able to contain. Thank him for the miracles that will take place over the course of your lifetime. Thank him for never leaving or forsaking you, despite all you've done. Watch God turn things around on your behalf.

NOTES:

January 9
Give Thanks Always

1 Thessalonians 5:18 (NLT)

Give thanks to God always. For all that he is and all that he has been to you. Thank God for sending his son, by which we inherit eternal life. Thank God for life, in which we live daily, saved by his grace and mercy. There is so much to be thankful for on a daily basis. Each day we wake up is a new day to praise the name of the Lord. No matter what you've experienced in this lifetime, God is still worthy of all the praise. There are numerous reasons that you should be praising the name of the Lord. We often take for granted who God is and what he has done for us, consistently. Take time out of your busy schedule to just say, "Thank you, Lord."

NOTES:

January 10
All Things Will Work Together

Romans 8:28 (ESV)

God promises a good outcome. No matter what you may be facing at this present time, God will make sure that all things work together for his good. This means that trials will turn into triumphs, if you allow God to be in control. Nothing that you go through is meant to hurt you. It's meant to strengthen you, to build your character, to build your faith in God and to help you rely not on your own strength or intellect. Things that are falling apart can really be falling together when God is in control.

Don't be so quick to underestimate the power that God has. His promises will not return to you void, his words will lead you to perfect peace, and what Satan means for evil God can turn it into good. Keep living.

NOTES:

January 11
Seek God Daily

Jeremiah 29:13 (ESV)

God has never left you, nor will he ever leave you. We often don't take time to seek out what God wants us to receive, but if we seek God, we'll find him every time. He is not hiding from us; we tend to hide from him. Whatever questions you need answered, whatever problem you need solved, whatever void you need filled, God is the one who will make it happen. There is nothing God can't do when you seek him with your whole heart. His hands are outstretched towards you; it's up to you to grab hold to the things God has and will lay before—this includes his presence.

Build an everlasting relationship with Christ. Be reminded daily that he is never too far away from you. Call on him, and he'll be right there for you.

NOTES:

January 12
Building A Solid Foundation

John 14:6 (NLT)

There is only one way to the Father (God), which is through his son (Jesus Christ). It's important to accept Jesus Christ as your Lord and Savior, so that you will inherit eternal life. There is no one in this physical world to save you—BUT GOD! Your outcome in life depends on your actions today. Start now building a relationship with Christ. A relationship that does not waiver, a relationship that can withstand anything, a relationship that is not swayed by the opinions of others, a relationship that is a priority in your life.

Jesus is everything that you're searching for. Building a solid foundational relationship with him allows you to see first hand what it means to be a true disciple of the risen Christ. Yes, he is spirit. But before you were flesh, you were connected spirit to spirit with the one and true living God.

NOTES:

Colossians 4:2 (GNT)

There is power in prayer. Prayer changes people and it changes things. The opportunity you receive daily to converse with God is very important to your growth and maturity. Don't just pray when everything is going bad, but also pray when all things are going well. Pray to keep from crying, pray to stay humble, pray to keep pushing forward, pray for strength, pray for courage, pray to see things the way God sees them, pray when you're happy and also when you're sad. Prayer is an effective and powerful tool needed in everyday life.

Be watchful, pay attention, listen and obey the commands God gives you during your prayer time. What the Holy Spirit says to you during prayer time should not be taken lightly. Be thankful that God has a conversation with you instead of just giving out mandates. Listen, then apply. God's instructions will never steer you in the wrong direction.

NOTES:

January 14
Patience Is A Virtue

Psalm 37:7 (NLT)

Learn to be patient. Practice patience on a daily basis. God does not work on your timing, so don't expect him to move when you want him to move. His timing is always perfect. You may wonder why things aren't happening as fast as you want them to. Just because you believe you're ready for something does not mean that you truly are. God takes his time in giving us what our hearts desire. Everything that comes from God is worth waiting for. Be still and know that he is God! God will never give you something prematurely; he cares too much about you to do that.

Trust the process, adhere to God's voice, be patient and work on God's timing. You'll be pleasantly surprised at the outcome. When God is all in it, there is no choice but to succeed. Thank you, Lord, for working it out.

NOTES:

January 15
Don't Give Up

Romans 8:16-17 (NLT)

Don't be surprised by the sufferings that you will endure in this lifetime. Christ endured so much for his children. What we will endure won't be anything that can measure up to what Jesus went through. Whatever you face, allow God to be your strength. You may suffer now, but your inheritance is in heaven. Your name may get slandered, you may be the outcast, you may think people don't understand you, and you may feel unloved and unwanted. But God! God can turn each negative day into a positive one, when you try him and obey his Word.

You are a child of God, co-heir to Jesus Christ. You will share in the glory that is eternal life. The suffering you'll face is preparing you for the blessings God will soon bestow on you. Don't give up!

NOTES:

January 16
Chosen By God

1 Peter 2:9 (ESV)

You are so important to God. God chose you! He set you apart and created you with a purpose. There is a purpose for your life, whether you've realized it already or not. There is something special about you, something that no one else possesses. The fact that God spent so much time creating everything about you makes you unique. Your uniqueness will lead others to Christ.

You were once in darkness, but God called you into light. Walk with purpose, remember who you're living for and share your uniqueness with the world, so that others are drawn to Christ through your testimony. Be a light!

NOTES:

January 17
The Right Direction

Proverbs 3:5-6 (ESV)

There should never be a day that goes by that you don't consult God in what you do. We often go through life's hustle and bustle, without consulting the one who makes all things possible. Just think, if we had consulted God how much smoother our days would be. There are things in life that you just don't understand—consult God. When you lean on your own understanding it will eventually lead to destruction, of some sort.

Don't you trust God? Will God lead you in the right direction? Isn't God's way, the best way?

The answers to the above questions will help you gauge if you're trying to lead your own life or if you're allowing God to lead you. You will need to submit to God's will and his way, wholeheartedly, in order to see better outcomes. Keep your life aligned with Christ.

NOTES:

January 18
A Life Of Peace

2 Thessalonians 3:16 (GNT)

God wants you to enjoy an abundant life of peace and joy. When you ask for peace, God will step in on the scene and become peace, in the midst of a storm. If you ask, you shall receive. You want peace on a daily basis? Ask God for that peace, a peace that surpasses all understanding. Two sure ways to bring peace into your life is by reading the Word of God daily and praying consistently. God will withhold no great thing from you, which includes peace. Speak peace into the atmosphere, and everywhere you step, peace shall be present, in Jesus' name. Keep your mind focused on Jesus and he will give you peace.

NOTES:

January 19
You Are Called To Love

Matthew 7:24-25 (NLT)

You were created to Love God and Love People. Sharing who you are and what God has done for you is how you'll reach others for the Kingdom of God. Everyone may not listen to you, but those who do shall be changed for the better. Remember that God is your foundation, the Bible is daily instructions and prayer helps you gain clarity. Put into practice everything you receive from God on a consistent basis. Someone is counting on you to help lead him or her to Christ. Someone is counting on you to give an encouraging word. Someone is counting on you to love him or her unconditionally, like Christ loves you. Don't be so into self that you can't recognize who God has placed in your life and for what reasons. Christ is doing a work within you. Stay steadfast and immovable.

NOTES:

January 20
Don't Be Deceived

Isaiah 6:10 (ESV)

Don't allow the enemy to trick you. He's tricky in such ways that we often fall for the traps that the enemy sets for us. He will put scales over your eyes so you can't see clearly. He will put plugs in your ears so you can't hear clearly. He will harden your heart, if you allow him to. But God! God is the truth and the light. God can allow all scales to fall off your eyes, so that you see with the eyes of Christ, so that you hear with the ears of Christ and so that your heart is pure like Christ's. It all depends on you. How long will you allow Satan to have his way in your life? How long will you put up with the schemes of the devil?

You have power over the enemy. Make sure that you are using the power and authority given to you by God. At the name of the Lord, Satan will have to flee. You possess a power through Christ Jesus, which Satan is afraid of.

NOTES:

January 21
The Change From Within

Ephesians 4:22-24 (ESV)

God will meet you right where you are. Don't think you have to change all your ways in order to accept Jesus Christ wholeheartedly into your life. He said to come as you are. The more you spend time with God, the more the spirit inside of you will change. Change starts from within and then it works its way outward. Committing your life to Christ means that you put off who you used to be spiritually, transforming your heart, mind and spirit to who God wants you to be.

God will change you and he will let you know the things that he wants you to change about yourself. Everything takes time, so enjoy the process. The more time you spend with God, the more you will want to be like him.

NOTES:

January 22
Unconditional Love

Isaiah 54:10 (GNT)

God is love! God has a love for you that is unfailing. No matter what you do, no matter what you say, no matter how many times you turn away from God, he still has unconditional love for you. It hurts him, but his love remains the same towards you. God is a forgiving God. There is nothing in this world that can amount to the love that God has for his children. Even when you don't feel loved by family, friends or your spouse, God's love still remains the same. Even when you don't love yourself, God's love for you still remains the same. Don't take God's love for granted. God's love for you doesn't come with stipulations; you don't have to give to receive it. God's love is the love that never changes.

NOTES:

January 23
Let The Holy Spirit Lead

Romans 8:26 (NLT)

Allow your life to be led by the Holy Spirit. There are a lot of things that you need help with on a daily basis—spiritually, emotionally, mentally and physically. The Holy Spirit is there to guide you on a consistent basis in the ways that you should go. In your weakness, the Holy Spirit makes you strong. The Holy Spirit will lead you to pray, even when you can't find the words to speak. The Holy Spirit will lead you to read the Bible when no one else has the answers to your questions. The Holy Spirit will speak positivity in your life when you thought you had lost all hope. Be sensitive to the Holy Spirit and allow yourself to be led daily, by the spirit of God.

NOTES:

January 24
The Right Timing

Psalm 55:17 (GNT)

God is just a prayer away. He hears your cries, pleas and petitions and he's working behind the scenes on your behalf. You may not know everything that God is doing behind the scenes, but he has it all under control. You're never going through anything alone; God is always right there. You may not always be able to feel God's presence because you've taken your eyes off him and placed your eyes on the situation, person or circumstance. As soon as you take your eyes off God, the problem seems as if it magnifies. But God! God has never taken his hand off the situation, he has never left you, he has never forsaken you and he has never stopped loving you.

God is an *on time* God. He will make all crooked roads straight, he will turn your darkness into light, and he will love you through your hopeless nights. Allow God to be your strength in the time of trouble, because he's always there.

NOTES:

Psalm 62:8 (NIV)

God is your safe haven. He's the only one that knows everything about you and still loves you, still protects you and still works for you. No one in this lifetime can be what God is to you. Not your mother, father, sister, brother, spouse, best friend, cousin, pastor, teacher, etc. So why not run to Jesus? He is truly the only one that knows everything about us and can help us better than we can help ourselves.

God wants you to trust him with everything; things that you are being challenged with, your deepest, darkest secrets, things you feel no one will understand, your weaknesses, your daily struggles, etc. Will you allow God to be your strength in areas where you are weak? Seek refuge in the true and living God.

NOTES:

January 26
Never Lose Hope

Isaiah 40:31 (ESV)

Don't lose hope. For when your hope is in the Lord, your strength will be renewed. Things may not be falling together like you hoped they would, but that doesn't mean that they aren't going the way God planned for them to go. Find strength in knowing that everything about your life is in the right hands—God's hands. Everything that God wants for your life will come to pass. It won't be in your timing, and it may not look exactly how you planned for it to look. But it will be a part of God's divine plan for your life. Find satisfaction in knowing that God has your best interest at heart and that everything will fall together the way God planned for it to be.

NOTES:

January 27
Inherit Eternal Life

Psalm 27:4 (GNT)

This life will pass away. Your goal should be to seek God daily so that you will dwell in the house of the Lord all the days of your eternal life. Your acceptance of Jesus Christ as your Lord and Savior means that you will inherit the riches of glory in heavenly places for eternity. While you're in this life you should seek the ways of the Lord and walk in obedience to him, seeking after the ways of Christ, being a great example for others to follow, sharing your testimony and being guided by the Holy Spirit. Heaven awaits you, and God has amazing plans for you.

NOTES:

January 28
Think Positive

Philippians 4:8 (ESV)

Frame your mind to think the way that God thinks. Is this a hard task? Yes. Can it be done? Yes. If you frame your mind to think on the positive instead of dwelling on the negative, your life will become positive. Have you ever thought of why you think about the things you do? God tells us to think on things that are true, noble, right, pure, lovely and admirable. All these things are positive things that God wants us to think about, yet our mind tends to think about more negative than positive things. There is a battlefield in the mind going on. You choose daily who wins and who loses. You have control of your thoughts. You can cancel out every negative thought with two or three positive thoughts.

Think on the things that God tells us will keep us focused on the positive aspects of life. Don't allow Satan to step in and grab your positive thoughts. His goal is to steal your thoughts, to kill your positive mind frame and to steal every positive thought you think. Don't allow Satan to win the battlefield in your mind.

NOTES:

January 29
The Perfect Protector

Psalm 91:1 (ESV)

God is your shelter, dwell in his presence all the days of your life. Allow God to be your protection, your shelter and your covering. When you allow God to be who he desires to be in your life, you'll see that things run smoothly. The moment you try to cover yourself, protect yourself or shield yourself, you'll find holes every time. Don't be so quick to think that you don't need help or think that you don't need a covering. God covers us even when we don't ask for it. We may not acknowledge his presence, but he's always there. Take the burden off yourself and rest in the arms of Christ daily, by ushering in his presence.

NOTES:

January 30
True Love

1 King 8:23 (NLT)

There is no God like the one true and living God. The love of God is like no other. No one can compare to him, no one in heaven or on earth. Many try to amount to who he is, but none compare to him. We are fortunate to know what true love is because we experience it daily through the love of Christ. We may not always recognize the love that flows to us, but God has his way of loving us. When you're not feeling the love, you should spend more time with Christ. No matter who, in the flesh, is not showing you the love you desire, know that you can always receive the love of your Father, God. He'll never disappoint you. Everything God does for you is out of love.

NOTES:

January 31
Change Your Thinking

Galatians 5:22-23 (ESV)

We tend to find ourselves thinking on things that are not like God, thinking about more negative things than we do positive things. God wants us to live a stress-free life, so why add more stress by thinking of all the negative things that have gone wrong or will go wrong. Think about things that are lovely; remember where your joy comes from and don't allow anyone to steal it from you; ask God for a spirit of peace that surpasses all understanding; ask God to give you patience so that you can do his will; be kind to everyone, even when you don't receive kindness in return; find the good in everything and be a great representation of Christ on this earth; be faithful to God unto death and you will receive the gift of eternal life; handle everything with care (circumstances, situations, people, etc.), and make sure you control your tongue, your attitude and your anger. God will make all things well. Lean on God like never before.

NOTES:

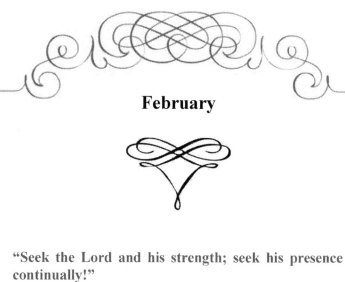

February

"Seek the Lord and his strength; seek his presence continually!"

—1 Chronicles 16:11 (ESV)

February 1
Power Over The Enemy

James 4:7 (ESV)

There is news for you—the devil will never stop coming at you. So don't be surprised at the attacks from the enemy. God is always in control. If you submit yourself to God, the devil will flee from you. Remember that you have the power over the enemy; he does not have the power over you. The more time we spend with God, the more equipped we become, and the harder it becomes for the devil to win the battle. We are in a spiritual battle daily, and we have the choice to fight or to give up. Today, don't give up! Use all the tools God has given you and never take the armor of God off. The devil is waiting for you to slip up. Lean on God and don't allow the enemy to catch you with your guard down.

NOTES:

February 2
Your Choices Matter

Romans 8:1-2 (ESV)

We are set free because of the blood of Jesus. We receive life in abundance through the precious Son of God. It is because of the life of Christ that we will inherit eternal life. Once you accepted Jesus Christ as your savior, you chose to live and not die. You chose your spirit over your flesh, you chose the narrow path instead of the wide path, you chose to put God first before yourself, and you chose the ways of the Lord over the ways of the world. There is life after death. You chose to believe in the one true and living God, the one who is the judge of all, and the one who makes all things well. You will inherit eternal life. You will live and not die.

NOTES:

February 3
Surrender All To God

Isaiah 12:2 (GNT)

Take refuge in the one true and living God; he can make all things well. God wants to be your strength in time of trouble. God wants to be your strength in time of sorrow. God wants to be your strength when you feel like you have nothing more to give. God wants to be your strength when you're down and out. When you put all your trust in God, he will make all things align with his will for your life. The moment God steps on the scene, he brings peace with him. Stop leaning on your own understanding. Trust God and allow him to build you up and strengthen you the way he needs to. The moment you surrender all to God, you will find out how real God truly is.

NOTES:

February 4
You're Stronger Than You Realize

John 16:33 (ESV)

Don't be surprised at what you will endure on this earth. For Jesus has already overcome the world. What you go through is not to break you, but to strengthen you in Christ Jesus. For in Jesus we find peace, in Jesus we find joy, in Jesus we find understanding. We won't ever have to endure what Jesus had to endure, but we will get a little taste of it. They hated Jesus, so why should they love us? Find peace in knowing that in the end, God wins. While we're going through it, God is behind the scenes making sure that all things are working in our favor. So find peace in knowing that the Holy Spirit is walking with you through the battle; he's walking with you through the hurt; he's walking with you through the pain. The best is yet to come; don't give up.

NOTES:

February 5
The Pilot Of Your Life

Psalm 105:4 (GNT)

We venture off course when we don't rely on God. We venture off course when we don't seek God on a regular basis. We venture off course when we try to do things our way. Aren't you tired of being off course? God wants you to continually seek after him like never before, so that he can show you how to stay on course according to his will. So take your focus off everything else and put your focus on God. Will you allow God to lead and guide you in the way that you should go? When you surrender to God you will find his peace and he will give you strength. Stop trying to lead yourself; that will only go so far before it leads to destruction. God's way will always lead you to eternal life. It's okay to allow God to be the pilot of your life.

NOTES:

John 14:27 (NLT)

There is no one that can do it like Jesus. There is not one person that can give life to you like Jesus can; there is not one person that can give peace to you like Jesus can; there is not one person who can give you clarity like Jesus can. Be reminded of who God is and what he brings when he steps on the scene. There are many blessings that Jesus bestows on us daily and peace happens to be one of them. You don't have to live in chaos or be around chaos. If Jesus lives in your heart and you are a child of God, you bring peace with you wherever you go. Don't conform to the circumstances; make the circumstances conform to you. Jesus wants you to experience peace all the days of your life; from this day forward, walk in purpose, walk in peace.

NOTES:

February 7
Aware Of God's Presence

Psalm 63:7-8 (ESV)

The help of God makes us want to continually cling to his presence because we know where our help comes from. There is nothing that God won't do for you. God has gotten you out of many tough situations. Many times you didn't know what the outcome would be and you asked for his help. God wants us to stay close to him whether we are in need or not. Cling to God's presence each day so that you will be aware of what is to come. Cling to God's presence so that you're not walking through life alone. Cling to God's presence so that you're not leading yourself. If you allow God's will to be done in your life daily, you will become aware of the ways he has made you the head and not the tail, above and not beneath.

NOTES:

February 8
The Guide To Life

Psalm 119:105 (ESV)

Get well acquainted with the Word of God, it is your guide for this lifetime. God wants to make sure that you are being consistently led in the right direction. If God's Word leads you, there is no question that you're going in the right direction. Without hearing from God, you're basically leading yourself. Even though you are unaware of what lies ahead, allowing God to lead you will only lead to greatness. Let God's Word penetrate your heart so that you are led daily in the ways of the Lord. Walk in purpose—God's will and not your way.

NOTES:

February 9
Be Light

Revelation 21:23 (GNT)

When God steps on the scene he brings light with him. That means that you as his child also bring light when you step on the scene. You can turn a negative atmosphere into a positive atmosphere. You can turn a negative situation into a positive situation, just by being light. There are plenty of dim places in this world that need the light of Christ. It is your responsibility to step on the scene and bring light with you, to brighten those dim places. Jesus is our prime example of what it means to be light. Allow yourself to follow the example of Christ so that you can be an example for others to follow.

NOTES:

Nehemiah 9:33 (NLT)

Thank God for being a God of another chance. We don't deserve all of the chances that we receive from God, yet he keeps giving us chance after chance to get it right. We act in ways that are not pleasing to God, and he still continues blessing us. Thank God for being a God of new grace and mercy. Each day we sin against God, yet God shows us favor. We turn our backs to God, yet he shows us unconditional love. God is faithful, God is just, God is perfect, God is all knowing, and God is all loving. Repent now of the sins you've committed against God. He's been too good to us. Thank you, Jesus!

NOTES:

February 11
A Way Out Of No Way

Matthew 5:3 (ESV)

God will continue to give you all that you need, if you continue to rely on him. Remember that your inheritance is not on this earth but it is in heaven. Where you lack, God makes up for it. So don't get discouraged. God is working behind the scenes on your behalf. God is making a way out of no way. God is making sure that you are not powerless but that you overcome all evil with good. Walk upright in the way of the Lord so that you can reap your inheritance. God promises to withhold no great thing from you. Stay on the potter's wheel.

NOTES:

Hosea 6:3 (GNT)

God desires an intimate relationship with his children. An intimate relationship requires spending time to get to know God like never before. God does not hide anything from his children. In fact, in spending time with him daily he will reveal the things that he wants you to know. Make it a daily habit to get closer to God. In doing so, you will have to eliminate distractions that keep you from spending time with him. Once you put in the effort, you'll see a transformation within yourself. God wants to do a new thing within you, and it will start when you commit to spending time with him daily.

NOTES:

February 13
You Are Never Alone

Psalm 21:6 (GNT)

Can you feel the sweet presence of the Lord? God is not hidden from you; if you seek his presence you shall find it. At times you get overwhelmed because you feel alone, but God is always near. You may even feel abandoned, but God has never left you. When you welcome God into your presence you will feel secure, you will feel peace and you will feel unspeakable joy. So ask yourself, have you ushered in the presence of the Lord lately? God wants to be near you, he wants you to be able to feel his presence and his love for you. Don't run from God, you'll never escape him.

NOTES:

February 14
Be Open To Receive

Deuteronomy 4:29 (ESV)

God wants you to seek him like never before. He wants you to be so in tune with him that you ask him to guide your next move, before you make it. When you seek God with your whole heart and soul, he will give you the desires of your heart. There is nothing that God won't do for you. God is an *on time* God. He holds everything in the palm of his hand. There is nothing too big or too small that God can't handle.

If you want answers to your questions, if you want things to move smoothly in your life, if you want the desires of your heart to actually come to fruition, you will need to seek God wholeheartedly with no stipulations, just an open heart and open mind to receive everything that he has for you.

NOTES:

February 15
God's Plan

Psalm 145:20 (NLT)

If you love God you will be obedient to everything that he has laid out for you to do on this earth. This requires time spent with God so that he can reveal what he wants you to do on this earth. God is very specific and everyone has an assignment on this earth. Just because you may not be aware of everything that God has planned for your life does not mean that there is no plan. God will reveal to you his plan for your life when you spend alone time with him. Those who aren't obedient to God will suffer the consequences. Stop trying to do things in your own strength; it will only lead to destruction. Allow yourself to do it God's way, which leads to eternal life.

NOTES:

February 16
Don't Be Confused

1 Corinthians 14:33 (ESV)

We will often have to make hard decisions in life. If ever there is a time when a decision needs to be made and you are confused on what needs to be done, have a conversation with Jesus. For God is not a God of confusion. The very powerless Satan comes to kill, steal and destroy by trying to make you confused about the critical decisions you need to make in life. Take a step back and always remember that confusion does not come from God, peace that surpasses all understanding does. So if ever you feel confused about anything, remember to have a conversation with Jesus and allow him to bring peace and revelation to the situation.

NOTES:

February 17
Let God Be God

Psalm 46:10 (ESV)

God is still God, no matter the situation or circumstance. So don't be discouraged that things aren't going your way, that things may not be in your favor right now and that you may not be receiving everything that you asked God for. Be still and let God be God.

Don't you trust that God has everything under control? Don't you trust that God is working behind the scenes on your behalf?

Be willing to wait on God so that he can reveal everything that you've asked of him. Be ready to receive everything that God has for you. Be open to change some things about yourself so that everything you want out of life will align with God's will for your life. Don't give up hope; God has it all under control. All God asks of you is to be still and know that he is God.

NOTES:

February 18
Encounter God Daily

Psalm 32:7 (GNT)

In the presence of God you will find peace. Allow your time spent alone with God to be your hiding place. In this place you will be able to limit distractions and actually hear the voice of God with clarity. In this place you can allow your heart to be free to receive what God has for you. You will only experience true freedom and deliverance when you encounter God daily with an open heart. Stop trying to hide from God; he's waiting for you to seek him like never before.

NOTES:

February 19
You Are Light

John 8:12 (NLT)

Once you have accepted Jesus Christ into your life you are no longer in darkness, but in light. With Jesus being the light of the world and you a disciple of his teachings and a child of God, you're also light. This means that when you step on the scene, you will change the atmosphere by being light. Always remember that you are to represent light in this world full of darkness. Don't ever allow your light to dim.

NOTES:

February 20
You Are Not The Judge

John 7:24 (ESV)

Stop judging others. We don't have the right to judge anyone, only God does. You may not like how others do the things they do, but that does not give you the right to judge what they do, because they are different from you. Take a peek inside your heart and figure out what needs to change in order for you to accept others the way they are. Never forget that God loves everyone the way they are. Remember that you do not sit on a throne and God does not give you the right to cast judgment on anyone. Check yourself before God has to check you.

NOTES:

February 21
The Narrow Path

Psalm 40:2 (GNT)

God rescued you from destruction. Once you made up in your mind, that this is the path you will follow, God continues to show you how great it will be. Stay on the narrow path that is less traveled, for it leads to eternal life. Be steadfast and immovable, never losing faith or hope in the one true and living God. God will make sure every crooked road is straight and every high hill brought down low for you. He will secure your every step, if you continue to rely on him. Don't give up on God because he will never give up on you.

NOTES:

February 22
The Rock of My Salvation

Psalm 18:2 (GNT)

Lean on the Lord and allow him to be your rock. God is there to hold you up when you feel you can't go on. God is your strength when you're weak. God is your shield in the time of trouble. God is your refuge when you want a hiding place. There is nowhere you can go to escape from his presence. Hold on to the Word of God and his promises for your life. He will never leave nor forsake you.

NOTES:

February 23
You Have Been Chosen

John 15:16 (ESV)

God has chosen you. Yes, CHOSEN! He chose you so that you can be a witness for the Kingdom of God. You will reach multitudes of people for the Kingdom of God. Don't think that you need to have it all together before you surrender totally to God. Just be willing to be shaped and molded daily by God. He will meet you right where you are and show you the individuals that you are to reach on his behalf. Don't disqualify yourself, because God qualified you and he chose you.

NOTES:

February 24
Born For This Life

Revelation 2:26-27 (NLT)

You are a conqueror. Whatever you do, don't stop being obedient to God. It may not be what everyone else is doing, but you're not everybody. It may not be what is popular right now—be the one that stands out from the crowd. It may seem like you aren't being rewarded for being a front liner for Christ—your reward is in heaven. You will soon reap the benefits. God has already made you the head and not the tail. You were born for this.

NOTES:

February 25
Give Thanks

Colossians 3:17 (ESV)

Give thanks to God. For everything he has done, everything he is doing and everything that he will do in the future. You have done nothing over the course of your life in your own strength. It may seem like you have, but every step of the way God has been with you. In everything you do make sure that God receives the praise, thanksgiving and the honor. God owes us nothing, yet he gives us everything.

NOTES:

February 26
You Have The Power

Revelation 12:11 (ESV)

You have the power over the enemy. He does not stand a chance against you. We often give Satan the power to rule over our lives, but he has no authority unless you give it to him. As a child of the most high you can defeat the enemy every time he comes at you. The blood of Jesus covers you all the days of your life. When you step on the scene, Satan has no power and he will flee. Remember the power that has been given to you by God and don't be afraid to use that power to defeat the enemy.

NOTES:

February 27
Shine Your Light

1 John 1:5-7 (GNT)

Walk in the love of God, sharing his light with the world daily. When you are in constant communication with God, he will reveal the people/places that need your light. Be ready when God tells you to move; it's crucial that you do what God tells you when he tells you. When your light shines bright, it attracts others to you, which then attracts them to God. It's not about you but about whom you will draw to God with your light.

NOTES:

February 28
Don't Take The Bait

Jeremiah 23:29 (NLV)

Be careful with what you hear and what you choose to obey. If it does not align with the Word of God, it is not truth. Be aware of false preachers and teachers; if their words don't align with the Word of God they're not truth. It is important to have your own personal relationship with God so that you know what he wants you to listen to and obey. Your discernment is vital. Make sure that everything you hear and choose to obey aligns with the Word of God. The enemy will send individuals to lure you off track. Don't take the bait.

NOTES:

February 29
Your Words Have Power

Matthew 12:37 (ESV)

Guard your tongue. For everything that comes out of your mouth can never be taken back. You will need to give account for everything you put out in the atmosphere, good and bad. So make sure that you think carefully and consider your words before you spit them out. Don't be someone who tears people down with your words, be someone that builds people up with your words. Make sure that the words you are putting into the atmosphere are pleasing to God. It is then that you will choose your words wisely.

NOTES:

March

"Study this Book of Instruction continually. Meditate on it day and night so you will be sure to obey everything written in it. Only then will you prosper and succeed in all you do."

—Joshua 1:8 (NLT)

March 1
Rely On The Word Of God

Matthew 24:35 (GNT)

God's Word will never return to you void. You can count on the earth passing away, but God's Word will never pass away. We need to rely on the Word of God, stand firm on the promises that God has given us and always remember who holds the key to all things. God doesn't want you to lose focus or to take your eyes off him. Allow God to reveal what he wants to reveal to you and to be taken to new heights in him. Believe the Word of God, live the Word of God and follow the commands that are given to you from God.

NOTES:

March 2
Faith Walk

Romans 10:17 (ESV)

Faith is the substance of things hoped for and the evidence of things not seen. This walk with Jesus is the best thing you could ever do. It's a walk that requires you to have faith in the unknown. By doing this you are continually blessed, because it shows that you trust God and what he wants for your life. There will be obstacles along the way that will attempt to make you lose faith, but don't. Remember who is in control and remember whom you're living for. Continue to walk by faith, knowing who is leading and guiding you every step of the way.

NOTES:

March 3
Don't Conform To The World

1 John 2:14-17 (NLT)

You are in the world, but you are not of the world. For anyone who loves the world, the love of God is not in him. You are set apart; God chose you. You may not be a part of the *in crowd;* God made sure that you stand out. It's perfectly fine that you don't want to do what you used to do, and don't allow anyone to make you feel bad about it. God will transform our heart and mind when we surrender to his will for our life. Don't be sucked into the things of the world, they will soon pass away. Stay on the path to righteousness that leads to eternal life in Christ Jesus our Lord.

NOTES:

March 4
God Is In Control

Luke 1:37 (ESV)

God doesn't have to prove anything to us, yet he proves that nothing is impossible with him. Whatever you ask in his name shall be done, if it aligns with his will for your life. Don't be afraid to ask God anything; nothing is too big or too small for him to accomplish. Make sure that for whatever you ask, your heart is in the right place. Be patient after you ask; God does nothing on your timing. You will receive everything at the appropriate time, when God knows that you are ready and prepared to receive it. God owes us nothing, yet he gives us everything.

NOTES:

March 5
Praise God Always

Hebrews 13:15 (NLT)

Take a moment to just praise God. We seldom take the time out to just praise the name of the Lord. Let today be the beginning of something new, praising God at all times. You know, God desires our praise and worship. Don't go to God asking for anything today, but try praising God today just for who he is and what he has done. Fill the atmosphere with your praises today. Bombard the heavens with your worship today. Get in the routine of praising God just because he's a good God, a God of another chance, a forgiving God, a God who loves you unconditionally, a God who sees past your faults, a God who is there for you no matter how many times you've turned your back on him. God is amazing, and he deserves your praises not only today but every second of every day.

NOTES:

March 6
Try The Spirit By The Spirit

Nehemiah 8:10 (ESV)

God will make all things well. He will give you joy for your pain, strength for your weakness and peace in the midst of your storms. Try the spirit by the spirit and allow God to show you who he truly is once you rely solely on him. God wants to make sure that no matter what you're going through you feel his presence. A sure way to feel his presence is to invite him in to your space. You should never want to go a day without experiencing the presence of God in your life and receiving direction for your life from him. Receive a clear revelation of what God desires for your life and start living it today.

NOTES:

March 7
God's Strength Is Powerful

Psalm 18:29 (GNT)

Your strength comes from God and God alone. You will know the difference between your own strength and the strength that comes from the Lord. Many things that can't be done in your own strength can be done with the strength of the Lord. God wants to build you up for his kingdom and strengthen you in ways only he can. Will you allow God to strengthen you?

You will be faced with battles that only God can get you through. You will be faced with trials that only God can turn into triumphs. You will feel like a victim in many cases, but God will assure you that you have victory. Don't give up hope today, but remember that your strength comes from the Lord.

NOTES:

March 8
God Is With You

Joshua 1:9 (ESV)

There is nowhere that you can go to escape from the presence of God. Even during the times that you feel alone, God is with you. When you feel that no one understands what you're going through, God is with you. When you feel like the weight of the world is on your shoulders, God is with you. There is nothing that you'll ever go through alone; there is nothing on this earth that you'll ever experience alone; there is nothing on this earth that you will face alone, because God is always with you. So today, be strong and courageous knowing that God has never left you and will never leave you. If you can't feel the presence of God, if you can't hear the voice of God, if you don't feel the love of God, guess who moved?

NOTES:

March 9
Reap What You Sow

Galatians 6:9 (ESV)

There is a harvest waiting on you with your name on it. You shall reap what you sow. Are you planting seeds in fertile ground? There is a season for all things. A time to plant, a time to water, a time to plow and a time to reap. There is a lesson for you in each season, so be content with the season that you are in. Ask God for clarity if you don't understand why you're there. You have to sow good seed in order to reap a great harvest. God does see your efforts, and he will reward you according to the seeds that you've planted in fertile ground. God hears your prayer and petitions, and he will not turn a deaf ear toward you. Stand firm on the promises that God has for your life. Your harvest shall be great. Don't give up!

NOTES:

March 10
Spiritual Warfare

1 Corinthians 10:21 (NLT)

There is a spiritual warfare going on daily. You have to keep your spirit saturated in the Word of God and prayer so that your mind, body and spirit do not give into the temptations of the flesh. Being a child of God, you have a target on you from the enemy (Satan). Satan is trying to kill, steal and destroy you by any means necessary. Your goal in life should be to do the will of God. You can't do the will of God if you so easily give in to the desires of your flesh. Remember that the more you spend time with God, the stronger you will be when it comes to fighting the temptations that Satan puts in your path daily.

NOTES:

March 11
Beware Of Satan's Schemes

James 1:13-15 (ESV)

Remember that any temptation that you give in to does not come from God; it comes from Satan. God can't be tempted by evil, and he does not tempt you with evil. Beware of the schemes of the enemy, for when you do good, evil is always present. You have to put on the armor of God to withstand the temptations of the enemy. You will be enticed by the things that are pleasing to the eye and that feel good to the flesh. But everything that looks good isn't good for you and everything that feels good is usually temporary. You have to make a conscious decision daily not to give in to the temptations of Satan; remember that he's not for you but against everything you stand for.

NOTES:

March 12
Set Your Mind On The Unseen

John 12:25 (ESV)

Be reminded daily that your life on this earth is just temporary. Your life truly begins when this life ends. Now, don't try to go out early. God has a purpose for you and you will fulfill your purpose and walk into your destiny before your life here on earth ends. So don't be so caught up in what this world can give you, be caught up in what life will be like for eternity. Set your mind on the things that are unseen (the heavenly realm) instead of on the things that are seen (this world), which shall soon pass away. Your life on this earth has no comparison to what life will be like in eternity. Live your life as if you want to see heaven one day.

NOTES:

March 13
A Disciple Of Christ

2 Thessalonians 2:10 (NLT)

Being a disciple of Christ is not always easy, but it is well worth it. Not everyone will believe in Christ Jesus like you do, not everyone will accept Christ Jesus like you have, not everyone will get a chance to experience heaven like you will. Many individuals will perish because they refuse to accept Christ Jesus as Lord. We do have a duty as disciples of Christ Jesus to be light in a world full of darkness, to love the unlovable, to be obedient to the Word of God, to stay saturated in God's Word, to share our testimony, to be of encouragement to those we come in contact with, to be in fellowship with other believers and to be an example of Christ in the world. It may not be easy, but this walk with Christ is well worth it.

NOTES:

March 14
Choose Life

Matthew 6:24 (GNT)

Each day you have a choice to make. Each choice comes with a decision and an outcome. Either God is your master or something else is. When God is your master, you've chosen life, and the outcome is eternal life in the heavenly realm. If you choose anything besides God as your master, you've chosen temporary gain and this leads to destruction. You can't serve two masters; either you'll love one and hate the other or you'll despise one and be devoted to the other.

Who is your master? Where will you spend eternity?

If you're reading this, you still have time to make a conscious choice to make God your master. Serving God will ensure that you get the best out of this life and the life to come in eternity.

NOTES:

March 15
Not Of This World

James 4:4 (ESV)

You're in this world, but you're not of this world. What this world has to offer you is nothing compared to what God has in store for you. The easiest route may seem to be doing what the world is doing, but the safest thing is to do what God has commanded you to do. You can't love the world and love God. You can't be of the world and do what God has called you to do; it's a conflict of interest. God makes living in this world so much easier when you adhere to his voice, follow his commands and stay rooted in his Word. You might fall short, but each time God is there to pick you up when you fall and push you to try again. God's grace is sufficient.

NOTES:

March 16
Receive What God Has To Offer

Mark 8:36 (ESV)

You long after so much in this life, but is it at the expense of your soul? It profits you nothing to gain everything you want on this earth, but never get a taste of heaven once you leave it. Don't be so consumed by having everything that looks good to the world; the world can't see your spirit, but God can. We feed, clothe and make sure that our outward appearance is up to par, but what about your spirit? Your spirit grows each day while your flesh is dying. We put so much emphasis on what the world thinks, but what about what God thinks? You know the world can't judge you, right? But guess who will? GOD. Don't forfeit your soul to gain this world, which has nothing but destruction to offer you.

NOTES:

March 17
A Constant Battle

Ephesians 6:12 (GNT)

Do you ever feel like you're constantly in a battle? Well, you are. There is a battle going on in the spiritual realm. This battle can only be won with the help from God. This means that you need to be equipped daily because this battle never stops. Guess what? Satan never quits and he never gets tired during the battle. But God! When you spend time in his Word, praying and meditating, God will prepare you for the attacks from the enemy. With God you can walk through the fire and not be burned. With God you can withstand any test from the enemy. With God you can win every battle. Don't give up; God will fight for you.

NOTES:

March 18
Be A Great Example

1 John 3:13 (GNT)

It should come as no surprise to you, that the world hates you. God's Word warns us of this. If they hated Jesus, they'll hate you, too. If they persecuted Jesus, they'll persecute you, too. So don't be offended that those in this world are against you. If they don't have a relationship with Christ Jesus, they may never understand your walk. They may never understand the passion or desire that you have to get closer to God each day. That's okay, just continue to be light in front of them, shower them with God's love and allow your walk to match your talk. Allow God's Word to be a lamp unto your feet and a light unto your path.

NOTES:

March 19
Be Equally Yoked

2 Corinthians 6:14 (NLT)

God ordains friendships as well as relationships. If you are unequally yoked, it will not last. This is why some friendships are never mended and some relationships don't work out. God will protect you from people that don't align with the will he has for your life. Whether you realize it or not, those who hinder your walk with Christ will be removed. Remember that God is a jealous God. If you're trying to hold on to someone, rely on God to show you whether he ordained it in the first place. Sometimes things fall apart so that better things can fall together. Stop trying to hold on to friendships or relationships that God is not in the midst of.

NOTES:

March 20
God Is Your Shield

Ezekiel 20:38 (ESV)

Those who come to bring destruction in your life will not prevail. It may feel like you can't catch a break, like people are coming at you from all angles of life. But God! Declare today that no weapon formed against you shall prosper. The darts from the enemy will hit you, but they will not penetrate. The attacks from people might shake you up, but they won't detour your walk with Christ. The persecution from friends and family may hurt, but don't allow it to make you revert back to the old you. God will help you to stand in the midst of chaos, to triumph through each trial and to be victorious no matter how victimized you feel. Through it all, God is still God.

NOTES:

March 21
Obey God

Psalm 119:115 (ESV)

It can be hard at times to keep the commandments of God. When you are obedient to God, you set yourself up for the many blessings that come from your obedience. It's not only being obedient to the commands of God, but also being obedient to those God has placed as authority figures in your life. Remember that obedience is better than sacrifice. God will make sure that if you do your part, he will surely do his. God is always doing something new within us each day. Adhere to what his command is for your life today. Make sure that you're being obedient to his Word so that you can experience all that God has for you.

NOTES:

March 22
God's Love Is Eternal

Psalm 103:9 (GNT)

God is a merciful God. He does get mad and sad when we make bad decisions, but his love covers a multitude of sin. So, no, God does not stay sad or mad long once we repent and ask for his forgiveness. So today, stop holding on to things that God has already forgiven. Things that you have buried so deep, even you'd forgotten it was there. God is not angry with you, so stop holding on to burdens that God wants you to get rid of. Each day should be a new day for you to get closer to God; in that he will show you what he dislikes, what he wants you to change and things he wants you to give up. God has a love for you that outweighs all sin.

NOTES:

March 23
Gods Masterpiece

Deuteronomy 7:1-6 (ESV)

God chose you. You didn't choose anything about yourself; God chose it for you. Everything about you was thought out by God and carefully created into perfection. God created you in his image, and you're perfect in his sight. There are many things that others may lack that you possess and vice versa. Be thankful that God created you in his image and perfected you in his sight; this means that you're one of a kind. There is no one in this world that is exactly like you (even if you're an identical twin). You should never feel less than you are, because God made you worthy. You should never feel unwanted or unloved because God made you in love, and he showers you with it daily. You were chosen by God to live this life; find joy and peace knowing God chose you for it.

NOTES:

March 24
Pay Attention

Acts 20:28 (GNT)

Pay attention to those who God wants you to encounter on a daily basis. There is a reason for you to be in the places you are on a daily basis. Take nothing for granted. God works in mysterious ways and he wants to use you daily.

Are you willing to be used by God in order to bring others to Christ?

God has given us a mandate, which is to love God and love people. In that, we will win others to Christ by sharing the love of God with others. There are individuals that you will encounter that will be led to Christ, through you. Don't be afraid to plant the seed. God will use you in a mighty way even you may not understand. If you want to be used by God, do it wholeheartedly, because God is ready to use you.

NOTES:

March 25
Adhere To God's Instructions

1 Corinthians 15:33 (ESV)

When you have a keen ear to hear God's voice and welcome his presence, you will seldom be deceived by the tricks of the enemy. Remember that Satan is a deceiver and he can just about use anybody to get you to go in the wrong direction. Once you realize the tactics and tricks of the enemy, you will surely identify who and what Satan uses to bait you. Don't be misled by those who come to corrupt what God is building within you. If you haven't seen it already, get ready for what is to come.

NOTES:

March 26
Your Role Is Essential

Ephesians 4:7-16 (GNT)

God calls for unity in the body of Christ. You are a part of the body of Christ. When any part of the body is not functioning properly, the whole body lacks. This means that whatever part you play in the body of Christ, you need to strengthen yourself daily so that you function properly. You may not realize, but the body of Christ needs you for the building of God's kingdom. You may not have it all together, but if you're at least trying, God will acknowledge that. Your role is essential; do the will of your father in heaven and help unify the body of Christ.

NOTES:

March 27
We Serve An Awesome God

1 Peter 1:8-9 (ESV)

Your relationship with God should never cease to amaze you. As you continue to build your relationship with God daily, you will find out new things about him. Remember that you're building a relationship, not just doing it as a religious activity. As you grow to love God more and more, your excitement about your relationship grows. You begin to believe in the still, small voice that you hear; you begin to have peaceful days, and you relax knowing that your joy is unspeakable and that his love is everlasting. It's a beautiful relationship that we often take for granted. In fact, it's the most important relationship that you'll ever experience.

NOTES:

March 28
Give God Praise Daily

Daniel 2:20 (GNT)

It makes God feel good when you praise and worship him in spirit and in truth. There is nothing wrong with having a praise break wherever you are—try it. It's important to give God praise daily, not for what he's done, but just for who he is. Don't you think that God deserves your praise? He's an amazing God. There are no words to actually describe how great he has been. Today, take a few minutes not to ask for anything but to just praise his holy name. Bless God today and forever more.

NOTES:

March 29
Don't Stop Doing Good

1 Peter 2:15-16 (ESV)

Everything that is good comes from God. Continue doing good, no matter who is watching. For by doing good, it will silence the ignorance of foolish people. Those who have talked against you will be silenced, those who spoke negatively over your life will be silenced, and those who said you'd never amount to anything, will be silenced. God will not allow anyone to hinder your process in doing good. Keep your eyes focused on Jesus, knowing that you will reap a harvest if you do not give up. Live a life that is pleasing to God, knowing that your inheritance awaits you.

NOTES:

March 30
It's Not About You

Philippians 2:3-4 (ESV)

This walk is not about you. It is about those who you'll touch along the way. You should count others more significant than yourself. This can be hard to do if you have a selfish mindset. Think about all that Jesus did for us when dying on the cross. If he had a selfish mindset, we would be in trouble. But he didn't; he thought about all the lives that would be saved by giving his life. It may be hard at first to be self-*less*, but God will show you daily how to die to self so that he can use you for his glory. It's a humbling experience to know that people are counting on you and actually need you to help them through this faith walk. It may get tough, but God will give you strength to endure.

NOTES:

March 31
Guidance From God

Luke 18:17 (ESV)

Come to God as an innocent child, listening to his every word and obeying each command. Always keep in mind that God created you, you didn't create yourself. You need God to guide you in the way that you shall go, being careful not to deviate from the path he has set for you. You don't know what's best for yourself, because you didn't create you. But God! God knows all things. Allow him to guide your steps even when it doesn't always make sense. You don't have to know the outcome, God does.

NOTES:

April

"Commit your work to the Lord, and your plans will be established."

—**Proverbs 16:3 (ESV)**

April 1
Stop Doubting God

Luke 18:7 (NLT)

Stop doubting that God hears you, because he does. God hears every prayer and petition that you lift up to him. He has not forgotten about you. God has not turned a deaf ear toward you. God shall prevail and your prayers shall be answered. In the meantime, instead of worrying, try praising and worshipping God. Not only for what he has done, but just for who he is. Today, don't lose hope. Today, don't lose sight of the promises that God will fulfill in your life. It's easy to give up, but it takes strength to continue pressing toward the mark. Allow God to be your strength today and keep pushing forward.

NOTES:

April 2
Serve Only God

Luke 16:13 (NLT)

Don't allow money to control your life; it is the root of all evil. You need money to survive on this earth, but you should never become a slave to it. Don't allow the enemy to trick you into serving money, for you can't serve God and money. You have a choice to make. You either serve God or you serve money, but you can't do both. You can go out and try to make things happen for yourself, or you can allow God to handle it, but you can't do both. Your way likely never turns out the way you planned, but God's way will always turn out better than you expected. So today, do yourself a favor and allow God to be your master and serve him wholeheartedly. It will be the best decision you'll ever make in life.

NOTES:

April 3
Holy Is The Lamb

Philippians 2:9-10 (ESV)

The name that is exalted which is the name above all names is Jesus Christ. You can't get to the Father but through our Savior, Jesus Christ. Every knee shall bow and every tongue shall confess that he is Lord. I urge you today to continue building your relationship with Christ. You may fall short at times, but never give up on your relationship with Christ. Think of how lost you'd be without his guidance, how lonely you'll feel without his love and how much darkness would overshadow your life without his light. Bless the name of the Lord.

NOTES:

April 4
Focus On Jesus

1 Peter 1:13 (GNT)

Keep your mind focused on Jesus. There is a battle going on and it's in the mind. This is why occasionally you have negative thoughts, you have lonely feelings, and you sometimes feel less than you want to be. The devil wants to keep you in bondage, and a sure way to keep you there is in your mind. You have the authority to take back your thoughts, anything that you think that is not like God. You can take back everything that the devil has stolen from you and is trying to steal from you now. This is your life; fight hard for it. The devil will never stop coming for you, so stay prepared.

NOTES:

April 5
God Has Never Left You

Genesis 28:15 (GNT)

God is with you. You may not always feel his presence, his voice may seem very distant from you and you may feel as if you're talking and no one is there. If you can't feel the Holy Spirit, guess who moved? If you're talking and can't hear a still, small voice talking back to you, you haven't waited patiently long enough. God promised to never leave us, which means he's always with us. Today, try not asking for anything, but take time out to listen to the Holy Spirit. Create a space to where God will embark his presence upon you, to where you are confident his spirit resides not only in you, but around you also.

NOTES:

April 6
Be Used By God

Matthew 28:20 (ESV)

You are to observe the Word of God and do what he has commanded you to do. A part of your purpose for living is to win souls for the Kingdom of God. God created you just the way you are, to reach the masses for his kingdom. All that you've been through in life is so that you can share with others who got you through those things. Even if you didn't recognize it then, God made sure that everything you've been through was not too much for you to handle. So stand proud, knowing that God wants to use you. The question is, are you willing to be used by God for his glory? Today, allow God to pour into you through prayer, reading the Bible and meditation so that you can pour into someone else what God has shared with you.

NOTES:

April 7
Born To Be Set Apart

Psalm 139:13-16 (ESV)

The creation of you was no mistake, because God has never made a mistake. God made you in his image and he created you fearfully and wonderfully, and wonderful are his works. So don't ever question your existence; you are not a mistake but a blessing to God. Before your parents knew they would conceive you, God already had a plan for your life. Before you knew why you were created, God already breathed purpose into you. God took his precious time to intricately knit you together in your mother's womb. Today, live with purpose knowing that you are not a mistake, knowing that God thought enough of you to create you and realizing that you have purpose and it's up to you to walk in it.

NOTES:

April 8
You Are Free

2 Corinthians 3:17-18 (ESV)

Freedom resides wherever the spirit of God dwells. Accept the spirit of God so that you can live, walk and breathe in freedom today. The devil tries so hard to put bait in front of you, to keep you away from God and his Word. Today, take back everything that the devil has stolen from you. No longer will he steal your time; no longer will you allow negative thoughts to stay; no longer will you be in debt; no longer will you hold grudges, but you will forgive; no longer will you harbor anger or ill feelings toward anyone; no longer will you be ashamed; no longer will you be in bondage; no longer will you believe the lies that people have said about you; no longer will you feel that you're not good enough. Today, God wants you to be free. Are you willing to be free today? Are you willing to allow God's spirit to live inside of your heart? This means that you will need to get rid of everything in you that is not like God. Live in freedom today and every day.

NOTES:

April 9
Live According To God's Will

Matthew 6:33 (ESV)

It's important to seek God in all that you do. Why? God has a way of showing you what he wants for your life. If you don't seek God, you'll never truly find what you're searching for. Remember that God knows all things. Every answer to every question that you've ever wanted to know, God has the answers. When you seek God with your whole heart, everything that you've ever asked for shall be added to you. It may not be on your timing, it may not look the way you thought it would, but it will be from God. All God asks is that you're obedient to his commands for your life, that you love God and love people and that you're faithful unto death. It takes discipline and dedication to live according to what God wants for your life; when you seek God you will find what God has in store for you.

NOTES:

April 10
For The Glory Of God

Colossians 3:23-24 (NLT)

Everything that you do in life should be done for the glory of God and not for men. Men can give you nothing that will last through eternity, but God gives you eternal life. Those who God has placed in your life as an authority figure, serve them as if you're serving God. Learn to not see the vessel but to see the spirit that has a need. God will place you on assignments that will allow you to build up leaders for the Kingdom of God. Don't take your ministerial assignments for granted. Wherever God needs you, he will place you there—a new job, a new house, a new church, a new school, a new organization, etc. God has placed you on an assignment in these places; be light and be an example of Jesus Christ while in these positions.

NOTES:

April 11
Adjust Your Focus

Romans 8:6 (NLT)

What is your mind focused on? You probably tend to focus on the matters of the flesh instead of the matters of the spirit most of the time. It's not uncommon to think on the things of the flesh, but it's not what God has called his children to do. God wants you to set your mind on the things of the spirit, for the things of the spirit are life and peace. To set your mind on the things of the flesh is death. You're not living just to die; you're living to experience heaven for eternity. Change what your focus is and you'll change your life. Allow the Holy Spirit to do a new work within you by transforming your mind and thinking on the things of the spirit, which leads to eternal life and peace that surpasses all understanding.

NOTES:

April 12
Consult Your Creator

Proverbs 20:24 (NLT)

If you didn't create yourself, how can you possibly know what's best for you? You need to consult the creator (God) of all things, so that he can order your steps. You will never know what God wants for your life if you never ask him. When asking God for his guidance and direction for your life, be prepared. Prepared that everything may not go as you planned it, prepared for the not right now, prepared for the facts that in order to get to step c you have to conquer step a and b. There is no easy route to get to where God is taking you. But if you stay on the path you will not be disappointed. God knows what's best for your life. You were created according to God's will and purpose.

NOTES:

April 13
Endure Until The End

2 Corinthians 4:17-18 (GNT)

The weight of the world might feel like it's on your shoulders right now. But God! God wants you to know that anything you endure on this earth is for a purpose. The purpose may be unknown to you, until you ask God why he's taking you through these trials, situations and circumstances. It is key to set your mind, heart and spirit on the things that will last forever (which is not your issues, problems or circumstances). When we set our eyes on things that are eternal (heaven, our spirit, God) we will begin to realize that we have to endure what we are going through, pass the test and learn the lesson before we get to our eternal destination in the heavenly realm. If you've never gone through anything you wouldn't need to rely on God and you wouldn't learn or grow into the person God intends for you to be. So rejoice in the Lord that he sees you through every trial and you come out stronger each time.

NOTES:

April 14
Wait With Expectancy

Psalm 5:3 (GNT)

Wait, expecting God to fulfill the promises that he has made to you. Every prayer request and petition has been made known to God. Learn to be patient, listen carefully and trust God with your whole heart, because your blessings and miracles are on the way. During this waiting period, start praising God for what you want to take place. This will put you in the position to receive everything that God has for you by giving God all the praise and glory that is due him. God will fulfill the promises that he has made to you.

NOTES:

April 15
Shift Your Focus

Psalm 37:25 (ESV)

There are miracles performed before your very eyes daily. How long will you keep your eyes on your problems instead of focused on the one true and living God, who can solve every issue? You're missing out on things around you because you're focused on the wrong things. What you will experience in this lifetime is nothing short of amazing. You'll enjoy more experiences if your focus in life is set on things that last forever, instead of on things that are temporary. Shift your focus today, to the things that will bring peace, joy and happiness to your life. Thank God for the miracles happening in, through and around you today. Embrace the unknown, knowing that God knows all things.

NOTES:

April 16
Born For A Reason

Galatians 2:20 (ESV)

You were not given this life to live it according to your will or purpose. You're alive to live according to the will of God and his purpose for your life. You have no clue how to operate your life, that's why you often find yourself in predicaments that only God can get you out of. Once you accept Jesus Christ as Lord of your life, you begin to truly live. When you allow God to take total control of everything about you, you'll begin to feel a peace that no one can disturb, a joy that no one can take away and a thirst that only God can quench. It's amazing to be a child of God. You've been granted access to the best gift given to mankind; his name is Jesus.

NOTES:

April 17
Use Praise As Your Weapon

Psalm 42:11 (NLT)

A sure way to get out of the turmoil you're going through is by praising God with your whole heart. Why? Praise is used as a weapon against the enemy. If you use it effectively you'll realize that your praise is truly your weapon. There is nothing that you'll ever go through that God can't fix. There is nothing that you'll ever face that God is not walking through with you. There is no health problem that can't be cured. There is no financial issue that can't be solved. There is nothing that you will ever face that God doesn't already know the outcome. Today, praise God for the outcome. What you're facing right now will not last always; God has a purpose for your pain. Life may not be easy, but God gave you life, live in abundance.

NOTES:

April 18
Heir To The Thrown

John 17:20-21 (NLT)

Jesus covers you that you may be strong and courageous in your faith. You are heir to the throne of grace and you are a part of a royal priesthood. What God has called you to do on this earth is to draw all men unto him. Because of you, someone will be drawn to Christ Jesus and saved. Every trial has been to strengthen your faith, every struggle has made you rely on God even the more and every test was set before you so that you can realize God qualified you for this journey. You may not know everything that God wants for your life, but know that you are chosen. God will use you to accomplish his goal here on earth, if you totally surrender all to him. Be a willing vessel and watch God use you in a miraculous way.

NOTES:

April 19
You Have A Ministerial Assignment

John 17:4 (ESV)

There is work to be done on this earth before your purpose is fulfilled. Just like a job, you have a ministerial assignment each day. To know what your assignment is, you need to consult God. It will be revealed to you who to reach and what their needs are. It's easy to do things your way, but God's way is better. Today, if you honestly want to be used by God to accomplish his work on this earth, you'll need to first surrender to God. Not your will, but his will be done today. Don't give excuses why you can't; be willing to give it your all and God will prove to you that you can.

God wants to use you. Will you allow him to use you for an assignment today? God's purpose for your life is better than any plan you have.

NOTES:

April 20
Total Surrender

John 17:3 (ESV)

True living is living a life that is pleasing to Jesus Christ. You haven't fully lived until you've built a relationship with Jesus so that you know what direction to go in life. If you're leading yourself, you're leading yourself to destruction. When you allow the Holy Spirit to guide your footsteps, that leads to life eternal. You may notice that your way is not working out too well, you've hit dead end after dead end. God wants you to surrender to him like never before, be willing to follow the directions of the Holy Spirit even when you don't understand it at times. Remember that God has your best interest at heart and he wants you to spend eternity in heaven with him. You have a choice to make, life with Jesus or death doing it your way. The choice is yours.

NOTES:

April 21
Be Transformed

John 14:17 (GNT)

The world doesn't understand the spirit of God that you surrender to. It's not for them to understand or make sense of. You know what God has called you to do on this earth; make sure that you are obedient to the Word of God. God has instilled in you his truth, his Word, his love and his light. Be transformed by the renewing of your mind and spirit each day, to carry out the plans that the Holy Spirit lays out for you. Don't be concerned about the world and what the world has to offer. The true and living God did not place you in this world to be like it; he placed you in this world to win souls to his kingdom. Allow God to use you to fulfill his will on this earth.

NOTES:

April 22
Peace Of Mind

John 14:26-27 (ESV)

There is a peace that God gives to his children when they accept him. The Holy Spirit gives peace that surpasses all understanding, a peace that withstands all chaos, a peace that the world can't give nor take away. If you haven't felt that peace, you haven't spent enough time with Jesus. Whatever is burdening you today, ask God to replace it with peace. Every void that you feel right now, ask God to fill it with peace. Jesus died so that you might have life. Enjoying peace on a consistent daily basis is living the life God has planned for you. I speak peace over your life and the situations you are facing right now, in Jesus' name.

NOTES:

April 23
Called To Greatness

John 14:20 (GNT)

You are a part of a royal priesthood. You live because first Jesus Christ lived. You are an example of Christ on the earth. The world can't see Jesus with their physical eyes but they can see an example of him on the earth, through you. You were born to share Jesus without fear. You were born to lead others to Jesus, which in turn leads them to Almighty God. Don't overlook why you were created, don't run from your calling and don't be overwhelmed by the will of God for your life. God has called you to greatness, he has anointed you for your purpose, in this life, and he has instilled in you his Word. You are fully equipped to do the will of God on the earth.

NOTES:

April 24
Shower God With Love

John 14:15 (GNT)

There are commands that God has laid out for us. In keeping these commands this shows our love for him. When you know better, you do better. If you want to show your love for God, following his commands is a sure way to show him that you love him. In order to know what his commands are for your life, you have to spend alone time with him daily. In that time of praying, meditating and reading his Word, he will reveal to you what his commands are. All you need to do from there is be obedient to his words for your life. It's that simple, yet we make it so complicated. God shows us his love on a daily basis, it's only right that we in return show our love to him by keeping his commands on a daily basis.

How will you show God you love him today?

NOTES:

April 25
I Will Trust You

Psalm 118:8 (NLT)

It is important to learn how to trust God with your whole heart, instead of putting your trust in man. If you haven't noticed, man will let you down almost every time. But God! God will never leave nor forsake you. Yet, we tend not to take refuge in God until we figure out that putting trust in man leads to disappointments, discouragement and destruction.

Today, can you rely on God for everything?

Remember that God knows all things and holds everything in the palm of his hand. There is a sense of relief knowing that we can take refuge in God and everything will work out according to his will for your life. With God, you're in good hands.

NOTES:

April 26
Don't Give Up

Psalm 118:14 (NLT)

The battle is not yours, it's the Lord's. Whenever you feel like giving up or giving in, remember that your strength comes from the Lord. Whenever you're down and out and can't seem to pick yourself up, remember that your strength comes from the Lord. When you feel weak and overwhelmed, remember that your strength comes from the Lord. Don't you dare give up! God has amazing things in store for you. During the battle, the Lord will fight for you. During the trial, the Lord will strengthen you. During the test, the Lord will encourage you. You shall be a conqueror; you are a part of a royal priesthood; you are the head and not the tail; you shall prevail in this life; you will defeat the enemy and you will inherit eternal life, through Christ Jesus our Lord.

NOTES:

April 27
Truth Is God's Word

John 12:48-50 (NLT)

The Word of the Lord is the truth. Not following the Word of God leads to judgment. We will all be judged on our actions, choices and decisions that we make. What is acceptable to you may not be acceptable to God. Be sure that you aren't tweaking the Word of God to fit your lifestyle. Allow your lifestyle to change to fit the commands of God. Following the Holy Spirit's lead on this earth will help you align God's will with your life. You can follow the commands of God, which lead to eternal life, or you can follow your plans, which lead to death/destruction. Align your life with God's will and you'll experience peace that surpasses all understanding.

NOTES:

April 28
Build A Firm Foundation

John 10:14-15; 27-28 (ESV)

When spending time with God you begin to recognize his voice, his presence and his anointing. God's will is that you follow Christ with your whole heart, like a sheep follows a shepherd. Once you accept Jesus Christ, you will not be left behind. You may go astray from the flock at times, but God will always welcome you back. The enemy will never snatch you from the hands of God, you will not perish but you will inherit eternal life through Christ Jesus our Lord. Your relationship with Jesus is essential for this journey you're on. Each day is a new day to build a strong foundation rooted and grounded in Jesus.

Will you begin to build a firm foundation today?

NOTES:

April 29
God's Love

1 Chronicles 16:34 (ESV)

God's love for you endures forever. There is nothing that you can do to make God stop loving you. Every time you went astray, God still loved you. Every time you disobeyed God, he still loved you. Every time you turned your back on him, God still loved you. Every moment that you didn't love yourself, God still loved you. There is an inexpressible gratitude that we need to offer up to God, for being a God of love. Even when we don't deserve his love, God showers us with his love. Today, bask in the love of God, even though we aren't worthy of his love, we don't deserve his love and we take his love for granted. God's steadfast love endures forever.

NOTES:

April 30
Seek And You Will Find

Psalm 119:9-11 (GNT)

When you seek what God has for your life, you shall find it. It may not look like what you planned it to be, but God's will is better than any plan you may have. A sure way not to go astray from God's Word and his will for your life, is by seeking him daily. If you know what God has in store for you, you won't veer off course. It's when we don't know what God's will for our life is, that we start planning the way we think it should go. That's leading yourself to destruction. Since you didn't create yourself, you can't possibly know what is best for you. But God! Allow God to shape and mold you daily and lead you in the way that you should go so that you don't depart from him.

NOTES:

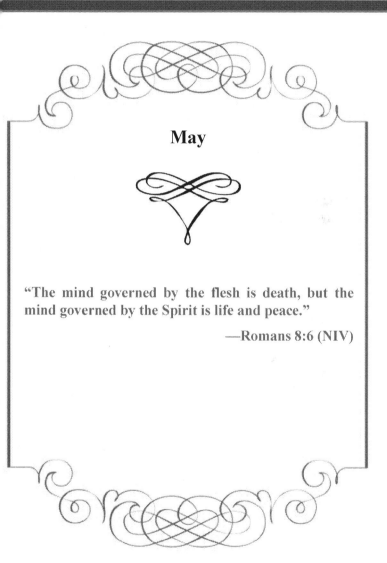

May

"The mind governed by the flesh is death, but the mind governed by the Spirit is life and peace."

—Romans 8:6 (NIV)

May 1
New Grace Daily

2 Corinthians 9:15 (ESV)

God's grace is sufficient. There is new grace and mercy given to you on a daily basis. Grace and mercy that we do not deserve, that has no price tag and that no one but God can give to us. We don't deserve it, yet God gives out this inexpressible gift repeatedly. We take it for granted yet he still gives it to us freely each day. What an awesome God we serve! Today, thank God for the free gift of salvation and the inexpressible gifts of grace and mercy. God loves you so much that his gifts last through eternity.

NOTES:

May 2
Power In The Name Jesus

John 6:47-48 (NLT)

There is power in the name, Jesus. It is only through him that you will inherit eternal life. It is only through him that you will receive salvation and be forgiven for your sins. Yes, Jesus is the bread of life, and only through him can you get to the Father (God). You must believe with your whole heart that he is the Son of God, that he died on the cross for your sins and that he was raised on the third day. Through Jesus, all things are possible if first you believe.

NOTES:

May 3
A Life Pleasing To God

John 6:40 (NLT)

You can't get to the Father (God) except through the Son (Jesus). God sent his son to die for you. Yes, you! You are so important to God that he wants you to spend eternity in heaven, with him. This life that you live is only a part of your purpose. How well you do on this earth determines your life in the heavenly realm. You have not seen or heard what God has in store for those who earnestly seek after him. So today, live as if you want to see heaven one day. For your life on this earth will soon pass away, but your life in heaven will last an eternity. God chose this life for you, live it in reverence to him.

NOTES:

May 4
Glorify God

John 6:37-38 (GNT)

God chose you for this life. No one can live it better than you. All the things that God wants you to inherit on this earth will come to you. You just need to make sure that it's being used to honor and glorify the name of the Lord, instead of glorifying your name. For everything that you receive on this earth is intended to glorify God. No matter how small or how big it is, no matter if it's in the spirit or in the flesh, everything is given to you to glorify the name of the Lord. Anything that is not being used to glorify God in your life will begin to be stripped from you. It's essential to use what has been given to you, by God, to glorify and praise his name.

NOTES:

May 5
He Is Omnipresent

Psalm 3:3 (ESV)

There is nothing that God won't do for you. He is there
for you every second of every day. When no one can be
found, he is there. When everyone turned their back on
you, he was there. When you couldn't do it alone, he
was there as your strength and your guide. Every trial,
God turned into a triumph. Although many times you
might have felt like the victim, God showed you that
you had the victory. During the test, God revealed to
you ways to endure. God wants to restore your faith in
him, to rebuild your relationship with him and to renew
your mind and spirit so that you can walk in the purpose
that he has for your life.

NOTES:

Proverbs 3:35 (NLT)

Wisdom only comes from God. If you aren't or haven't been walking in the way of the Lord you will be put to shame. There is a great calling on your life, and to fulfill the promises God has for your life you will need to use wisdom. Remember that you were given this life, but it's not about you. You will need to know what to do next—that requires wisdom. You will need to know who to reach—that requires wisdom. You will need to know what to say—that requires wisdom. You see, everything that we say and do on this earth requires wisdom. If every step you take is not based on the wisdom given from God, how will you know if you're stepping in the wrong direction? When you consult God, you'll begin to see his hand in everything.

NOTES:

May 7
Trust With Your Whole Heart

Proverbs 3:1-2 (NLT)

It's important to trust God with your whole heart. In trusting him you begin to build a solid relationship with him. In building this solid relationship you begin to learn the ways of the Lord. In learning the ways of the Lord you will begin to hide them in your heart so that they are stored there. God's Word being stored in your heart will eventually overflow and come through your mouth. Out of the abundance of the heart, the mouth speaks. Continue to work daily on building a solid relationship with Jesus, one that is built on love, faith, discipline and obedience. In this, you will begin to live a life that is pleasing to God.

NOTES:

May 8
Treat Others Fairly

Proverbs 3:3-4 (GNT)

Don't forsake what was instilled in you as a child. Learn
to treat others not how they treat you, but the way God
treats you—with loyalty, kindness, forgiveness and love.
In doing this, it will please God and it will change hearts
in those you come in contact with. You don't have to
treat others unfairly because they treat you unfairly. You
should forgive others even if you think they don't
deserve forgiveness. You should love despite feeling the
person is unlovable. Jesus is our example. If you follow
the example of Christ you will find favor with God and
people, and you will earn a good reputation that is
pleasing to God.

NOTES:

May 9
Use Discernment

Proverbs 13:20 (ESV)

It's important to recognize the company that you keep. "Birds of a feather do flock together." If the company that you keep isn't going in the right direction and you're following them, you all are being led astray. It's important to keep company with the wise so that you can become wise. For if you make friends with fools you will be ruined. Consult God in all that you do, so that he will pour into you the wisdom that you need to make the important decisions in your life. Who you surround yourself with has everything to do with how far you will go in life. Choose individuals that God chose for you, individuals that will uplift you instead of tearing you down, individuals that are going in the same direction that you are going.

NOTES:

May 10
A Willing Vessel

John 4:34 (ESV)

There is work to be done on this earth. You are one of the vessels that God will use to complete his work on this earth, only if you are willing. You were created for such a time as this. To bring light to darkness, to bring life to a dead situation and to be of encouragement to someone in need. Your trials didn't break you. Your test made you stronger. Your best days have yet to come. Allow God's Word to be your food, and as you devour it, walk in the truth of God's Word. Allow prayer to be your weapon against the enemy, war in the spirit as you pray and give thanks. You are worthy to be used by God, and God wants to use you for his glory, on earth.

NOTES:

May 11
Worship In Spirit And In Truth

John 4:24 (ESV)

Not everyone will worship God, but those who do must worship him in spirit and in truth. When you worship God, your spirit bears witness to the Holy Spirit, in truth. So don't be afraid of receiving the Holy Spirit and his anointing daily. This will give you the power to endure what you go through as well as allow you to share Jesus with others. It is important to hide the Word of God in your heart daily because it is truth. Individuals will not only be listening to you but they will acknowledge the Holy Spirit that resides in you. Be steadfast and immovable, relying on the truth of God and walking in obedience.

NOTES:

May 12
Joy Unspeakable

Psalm 37:4 (NLT)

The world can only give you temporary happiness. The joy that comes from God is eternal. Your goal in this life should be to seek what God has for you. When you seek God with all your heart, he will give you the desires of your heart. Nothing in this world is as important as what God has in store for you. The only way to know what God has in store for you is by spending time with him daily. Not only praying to him and reading his Word, but also listening and being obedient to his instructions for your life. It's important to develop an authentic relationship with the God you love and serve. What the world gives will be taken away. What God gives will last through eternity.

NOTES:

May 13
The King Of Kings

Psalm 145:21 (NLT)

What a mighty God we serve. There is power in the name, Jesus; every knee shall bow and every tongue shall confess that he is Lord. Once you build your relationship with Jesus, you'll begin to realize that there is no one like him. There are no words to express how amazing he is, there are no awards that can amount to his glory and there is no monetary value to compare to his greatness. Every day of your life should be spent praising the name of the Lord; he is that good. Not everyone will understand your praise because we all experience God in different ways. All God asks is that you continue to praise and worship him daily. Through your praise and worship you will feel the love of God like never before. Allow your praise and worship to be real.

NOTES:

May 14
Salvation Through The Son

John 3:17 (NLT)

Jesus came into this world to save the world, not condemn the world. If ever you feel condemned know that it comes from the enemy—condemnation does not come from God. God forgives you when you repent. The enemy continues to remind you of what God has forgiven of you. Don't be tricked by the enemy and his tactics. God sent Jesus to die on the cross for your sins so that you will have freedom through Christ Jesus, our Lord. You may fall short of the glory of God, but you are back in right standing when you repent and ask for forgiveness. Don't beat yourself up over the things that God has already forgiven you for. The blood of Jesus Christ covers you. Believe it and receive it in Jesus' name.

NOTES:

May 15
Be Used For The Greater Good

John 3:16 (ESV)

God loved you so much that he sent his only son to die for your sins so that you could receive eternal life. That alone should give you the desire to serve God all the days of your life. We could never love God as much as he loves us. But we do have the opportunity to spend our lifetime taking up our cross and following Jesus. Allowing what we do and who we are to exalt the name of Jesus, we can enhance our relationship with God so that we are an example of him on the earth. We owe it to God to be light in this world so that we can draw all men unto him. God created you to be used for his will and his glory on this earth.

NOTES:

May 16
Know Better And Do Better

Psalm 119:11 (ESV)

Each day is a new day that God allows you to be on this earth, to receive what he has for you. It is essential to store his Word in your heart so that you don't sin against him. When you know better, you do better. God is constantly trying to teach you his ways so that you don't depart from them. There is nothing that saddens God more than you not being obedient to his Word. Have a willing heart to obey the commands that God sets out for you daily. Remember that God has your best interest at heart. What he wants for your life is nothing short of amazing. But in order to get to where he wants you in life, you will need to surrender your life in turn for the life that he wants for you. When you're obedient to the Word of God, he will give you the desires of your heart.

NOTES:

John 5:30 (ESV)

Once you give your life to Christ, your life is no longer your own. You begin to have the desire to do God's will instead of doing things your way. You begin to realize your purpose and take steps that lead you to fulfill it. Your walk becomes different, your talk becomes different, your outlook on life is transformed and your heart begins to change. Having an authentic relationship with Christ needs no validation. God will meet you right where you are. Things will not happen overnight for you. The moment you give your heart to God and allow him to mold and shape you, is the moment that you will begin to feel the transformation from the inside out.

NOTES:

May 18
Life Through Jesus Christ

John 5:24 (ESV)

There is no way to get to God but through Jesus Christ. If you can't acknowledge the Son, you will not have access to the Father. It's essential to build a solid relationship with Jesus daily. A relationship that is not solely based on what he can give you, but based on the fact that he created you and you were created to praise, worship and exalt his name daily. You are to hide God's Word in your heart so it does not depart from you, you are to love the unlovable, you are to forgive the unforgiveable and you are to lead individuals to Christ just by being who God called you to be. If you've wholeheartedly given your life to Christ, you will experience the greatness of eternal life through Christ Jesus our Lord.

NOTES:

May 19
Abundant Life

John 5:22-23 (NLT)

God has given authority to his son, Jesus, to bring about judgment on the earth. Although that was not God's objective when sending his son to die for you on the cross. Jesus died that you may have life and have it more abundantly. In all that you do, your life should honor God. In all that you do, it should be pleasing to the eyes of God. This is why your relationship with Jesus needs to continue to be built daily; the closer you become with Jesus the more you will want to be like him. The more you become like Jesus, the more your mind, body and spirit will reflect the God you serve. Live a life worth living and in all that you do let it be pleasing to God.

NOTES:

May 20
Have a Keen Ear

Isaiah 30:21 (ESV)

It's not hard to hear the voice of God, you just need to take time and listen. If you aren't spending enough time listening for the voice of God, he could be speaking and you'll miss his voice. If you're so concerned about getting your desires met, your questions answered, or if you don't know when to stop talking, you'll miss the voice of God. God is not silent. You just haven't taken the necessary time out to listen. It's crucial to spend time with God daily so that you can hear his voice. In hearing God's voice you will hear his commands, his direction for your life, confirmation about what you've been asking and revelation on things that weren't always clear to you. Take time out today just to listen to what God has to say to you. Don't be afraid, God has your best interest at heart.

NOTES:

May 21
Authentic Life Journey

Ecclesiastes 12:13 (ESV)

There is purpose behind your birth. God created you to serve him, honor him and fear him. Amongst these things, God has laid out commands for you to follow until you meet him in heaven one day. It's not stressed enough in today's society how important life with Christ Jesus truly is. It's not a religious activity. A real authentic relationship with Christ is needed for this journey through life. Why? God created you; you didn't create yourself. You can't possibly know everything that you're supposed to do on this earth. But when you build your relationship with Christ, he'll give you instructions. If you follow those instructions daily, you'll have a life worth living. God knows all things even before they take place. So he can surely tell you what, when, why, where and how to do the things that he has called you to do on earth.

NOTES:

May 22
Perform The Miraculous

Ephesians 3:20-21 (ESV)

God is able. Anything that you can ever ask or think can be done in the name of Jesus. There is nothing too great that can't be accomplished by Almighty God. From the depths of the earth to the highest peak, God is able to do the miraculous. You've seen God work numerous times in your life, from the smallest blessing, to the largest miracle. What is impossible with man is possible with God. It's when we really turn our fears into faith that we become a witness to the works of God. It's when we turn our worries into trusting God wholeheartedly that we begin to see the impossible become possible. God wants to show up and show out in your life. Are you willing to take a leap of faith? Will you trust God, expecting him to move in ways that seem impossible? God wants to do a new work in and through you.

NOTES:

May 23
Live By Faith

Jude 1:20-21 (NLT)

Faith makes things possible. Whatever you're believing God for right now will manifest itself if it is a part of God's will for your life. You need faith in order to endure everything that you will face during this lifetime. Things may get rough, tests may seem unbearable, trials may seem as if they will never end. But God! All God asks of you is to trust him. Remember that God is the only one that knows the end at the beginning, God is the only one that can tell you the right way to go, and God is the only one that can make the impossible possible. Believe God for everything that you have been asking him for; expect it to come true by faith. While you're waiting, praise God, thank God, spend time with God, be obedient to God's commands and then watch God work. God will withhold no good thing from his children—he promised that to you.

NOTES:

May 24
God's Plan

Jeremiah 29:11 (NIV)

It's important to know the plans that God has for you. Every plan for your life that God has is good. God's plan for your life will never fail. Remember that God knows all things and can see all things. You may have plans for your life, and you may think that you have everything mapped out. But does your plan line up with God's plan? The only way you'll know if both plans are on the same accord is if you talk with him. You have to be willing to abandon your plan and pick up where God wants you. Knowing that what God has in store for you is better than anything you have for yourself. Let him be the driver in your life and you the passenger. Your life has purpose, and God wants you to walk in the destiny he has planned for you. Not on your timing but on his timing, not by following your own rules but by following his rules, and not by listening to your conscious but by obeying his voice.

NOTES:

May 25
Exalt The Name Of The Lord

1 Chronicles 29:11 (GNT)

It's sad that we know who God is, we know what God is capable of, we know what he has done for us, and yet we don't give him enough praise, glory or honor that is due his name. There is no one on earth or in the heavens that is more important than God, yet we place so many people before him. There is nothing so great that it can compare to God alone, yet we place so many things as idols (consciously and unconsciously). God is a gentleman. He will not force you into a relationship with him. As many times as you've turned your back on God, made him seem unimportant, acted as if he didn't exist, he was there with outstretched arms, a forgiving heart and a love that covers a multitude of sin. Today, praise God in your own way, just for being a faithful, trustworthy, loving, forgiving, omnipresent God. God is worthy to be praised, and he wants your praise and worship today.

NOTES:

May 26
Pray With Expectancy

Daniel 4:3 (ESV)

God wants you to expect him to do the things that he has placed in your heart. Those things that you have no idea how they will take place, those things that you can't see with your natural eyes right now, those things that people have told you are impossible, those things that you've prayed for and put your hope in. You shall see signs, you shall see wonders and you shall see miracles take place when you believe. God has not placed those things in your heart for nothing. This is where real faith comes into play, believing God for the impossible and believing that all things are possible with God. God is excited for your future. As soon as you start praying with expectancy, you'll see things start to move in your favor. God is up to something.

NOTES:

May 27
First, You Have To Believe

Luke 18:27 (ESV)

The Holy Spirit is going to show up on your behalf. The impossible will be done in your life if first you believe, remembering always that what God can do, no man can accomplish. But with the help of God, all things are possible. Do you truly believe that God can do the impossible? If not, start believing today that God will do miracles in you, through you and around you. Your faith, your discipline, your obedience and your time spent with God will bring to fruition everything that God has in store for you. With God, anything is possible. Today, thank God for all that he has done, all that he's doing and will do on your behalf in the future. Your breakthrough is on the way! Your miracle is on the way! Your blessings are on the way! Believe that God can, and he will make all things work together for his good.

NOTES:

May 28
Alpha And Omega

Exodus 15:2 (NIV)

God is…the alpha and the omega, the beginning and the end, the comforter, the defense attorney, the lover, the great *I am*, the teacher, the deliverer, the giver of life, the giver of salvation, the true and living God. So much to be said about God, yet words are not enough to express the greatness he possesses. If you have yet to truly experience the greatness of Jesus, start today. If you desire a better relationship with Jesus, start fresh today. God will meet you where you are. It's up to you to stay disciplined in building your relationship. Be steadfast and immovable and don't give up on God because he will never give up on you.

NOTES:

May 29
Don't Lose Hope

Hebrews 10:23 (NLT)

Hold on to your hope. God has promised you some things; he has put hope in your heart; he has put dreams in your heart and visions in your mind. No one has to understand them but you. No one has to believe them in order for them to come to pass but you. No one has to help them manifest, but you. No one has to know about them but you. When God plants that hope in your heart, don't let it just sit, do something about it. Pray on it, fast for it, speak it into existence and go for it. You can do all things through Christ that strengthens you.

How big is your hope? How big is your faith? Trust in the Lord with your whole heart and don't lose hope.

NOTES:

May 30
Seek God's Plan

Jeremiah 29:12-13 (ESV)

When you seek God with all your heart, you'll find him. Stop looking for everyone to solve your problems. Stop looking for everyone to give you answers to the questions you desire. Stop looking for just anyone to fill those voids that you're feeling. God is the problem solver. God holds every answer, to every question that you can think of. God wants to fill those voids with his spirit so that you will feel complete. God wants amazing things for your life. God's plans are not your plans or his thoughts your thoughts.

When you aren't feeling loved, seek God. When you aren't feeling worthy, seek God. When there is no one to talk to, seek God. When you think no one will understand, seek God. When you're having a bad day, seek God. When you're having an awesome day, seek God. During the trials, seek God. During the triumphs, seek God. Your ultimate daily goal, should be to seek God with your whole heart.

Stay steadfast and immovable and allow God to show you his will for your life according to his riches in glory.

NOTES:

May 31
Forgiveness Is Freedom

Zephaniah 2:3 (GNT)

It's important to ask God for forgiveness daily. To confess the things that you've done that were not pleasing to him, that did not glorify his name and that is against what he represents. We sin daily and there is no way to get around that. So it's up to you to repent and get back in right standing with God. God loves a pure heart, a humble spirit and those who walk in obedience to his Word. Continue to pour out your heart to God daily, this will bring freedom to you and put you back in right standing with God.

NOTES:

June

"So be strong and courageous! Do not be afraid and do not panic before them. For the Lord your God will personally go ahead of you. He will neither fail you nor abandon you."

—Deuteronomy 31:6 (NLT)

June 1
Strength In The Time Of Trouble

1 Chronicles 16:11 (ESV)

The enemy is after you, but God is your strength and your help in the time of trouble. God has chosen you for the life you live. It's not a coincidence that you're going through what you're going through. God knew that you were strong enough to endure through the journey. When you get overwhelmed remember to seek God for comfort and strength. When you feel burdened, seek God and cast your cares on him. When you feel like life is too much to handle, seek God for direction. When you get tired of doing good, seek God and allow him to show you the promises he has for you if you don't give up. When you stay in the presence of God, all day, every day, you will find peace that surpasses all understanding. Seek ye first the Kingdom of God and his righteousness and all things shall be added to you.

NOTES:

June 2
Pursue Peace

Psalm 34:14 (ESV)

When you do good, evil is always present. This does not mean that you have to give in to the evil that resides all around you. Seek peace and pursue it. Seek God and find refuge. Seek love and find God. God will help you in the times that you need to make the decision whether to give in or walk away. There is no situation that God places you in, where you're not given a choice. There is always a choice to make in life. You need to focus on what God wants you to do, instead of your sinful desires. Everything that looks good and sounds good is not always good for you. The more you spend time seeking God, the more you will find ways to stand strong against the enemy and his tactics.

NOTES:

June 3
This Life Was Chosen For You

2 Timothy 4:17-18 (NIV)

God chose this life for you. The attacks that you are experiencing are an indication that you're doing something right. The enemy would not be attacking you if you were not doing the will of God. It may seem like God is nowhere to be found, but the teacher is always the quietest during the test. Can you rely on God during the struggle? Your breakthrough is right around the corner. God not only chose you for this journey and for this life, but he also anointed the outcome and has aligned it with his will for your life. If you knew the end at the beginning, you wouldn't appreciate the process. God knows the end at the beginning, and as you rely on him and seek him daily he will help you endure through the journey with peace and joy.

NOTES:

June 4
Crown Of Glory

2 Timothy 4:8 (NLT)

Live as if you want to see heaven one day. There is a crown of life that awaits those who have accepted Jesus Christ as Lord. Your time here on earth is just for a little while because your riches in glory reside in the heavenly realm. What you've been learning during this life shall prepare you for what eternity has in store for you. What awaits you is far better than anything you can ever ask for or think. Stay faithful unto death and you will inherit eternal life.

NOTES:

June 5
No Limit On Love

1 Corinthians 13:2 (ESV)

Love bears all things, believes all things, hopes all things and endures all things; love never fails. Stop putting a limit on your love for others, let love guide you, let love help take off the blinders, let love break down walls, let love help remove bondages. Love will never fail you. God is love and God will never fail you. Today, put away selfish ways, put away selfish desires, put away ungodly thoughts and actions. Today, love for real. Someone needs your love and someone is counting on your love. So love with no limit, love with no strings attached, love more than you dream, love more than you hope, love more than you have faith. Love sees no faces; learn to love for real.

NOTES:

June 6
Strong Enough To Endure

Hebrews 4:16 (ESV)

Jesus knows what you're going through. Don't think for one second that he doesn't sympathize with you. Remember when Satan tried to tempt Jesus? Never did Jesus give in, never did he give up, and he's the only person that walked this earth sinless. Jesus sympathizes with you and his grace and mercy are sufficient. You have weaknesses, you will fall short of God's glory sometimes, but you can't give up. Try not to give in, and recognize who and what Satan tries to put in your way to get you off course. Remember that Satan was once an angel; he wants you to be as miserable as he is. Draw close to God and God will draw close to you. Stay focused on God's plan for your life.

NOTES:

June 7
Match Your Walk With Your Talk

1 John 2:4-6 (ESV)

Make sure that your walk and your talk match one another. People will not believe you if you say one thing but are living an opposite lifestyle. Be careful, for before your words come out of your mouth, people are watching your actions. If the Word of God resides in your heart, your actions will match them. For out of the mouth, the heart speaks. Make sure that who you say you are, what you stand for and who you are trying to become all align with Gods purpose for your life. Allow God to shape and mold you daily into the person he created you to be.

NOTES:

June 8
Don't Conform

1 John 2:15-17 (GNT)

You were not placed in this world to be like the world. You are in the world, but not of the world. Don't love the world or what the world has to offer. Remember that the world is Satan's playground, and he's out to entice you with things that are not of God and that don't represent God. Make sure that you are paying attention to the tactics of the enemy. When you know better, you do better. Any desire of the flesh, desires of the eyes and the pride of life are traps of the enemy to get you off course. Allow God to be your strength in the areas that you are weak. Allow God to fill any void with his presence. Allow God to saturate you with his anointing. The blood of Jesus covers you.

NOTES:

June 9
Growing In The Spirit

1 John 2:24-25 (ESV)

You have the tools needed to get through this life and to experience eternal life through Christ Jesus. God continues to equip you daily when you pray, read his Word, meditate on what you hear and be obedient to the will of God. It's essential to hide the word of God in your heart so that it will not depart from you. You've been trained up until this point, and the Holy Spirit will continue training you in the way you should go. Pray, listen and be obedient. Your life is not your own. God will use you if you avail yourself to his Word and to his will. It all begins with what you've learned and how you'll apply what you've learned in your life. God has made no mistake in choosing you for his kingdom.

NOTES:

June 10
Continue Doing Good

Hebrews 10:35-36 (NLT)

Don't stop doing good. God has called you to put all your trust in him, to step out on faith even when you don't see the outcome. God has put inside of you something that others may not identify with. God has put inside of you something that others may not understand. God has put inside of you something that will bring individuals to the Kingdom of God. Continue to walk in the confidence that God has given you. Don't doubt what God can, and will do, through you. God has called you to something greater. Accept the challenge, knowing that the outcome will be great. You may have to walk alone at times, you may not feel accepted at times and you will have to get out of your own way. But God! God is leading you through this journey. Don't forget to thank him for giving you endurance and pushing you to the next level. The outcome will be worth it.

NOTES:

June 11
God Is Able

2 Corinthians 4:8-10 (NIV)

Endure despite what you're going through. Remember that God is able to do exceedingly above anything that you can ask or think. God gave you an example of what you would endure on earth through the illustration of the life of Jesus Christ. If you are experiencing pain, hurt, persecution, affliction or despair right now, remember that God will give you endurance to get through it. Never doubt that God chose you for this life. Never doubt that God has a purpose and a plan for what you're facing. God will give you strength through the pain, peace through the hurt, courage through the persecution, clarity through the affliction and joy in despair. Expect God to move even when there are obstacles standing in the way. Trust God through the process.

NOTES:

June 12
Being Strengthened Spiritually

2 Corinthians 4:11-12 (ESV)

Each day you are living, your body is dying, yet your spirit is being renewed. Don't be so caught up in what your fleshly body can do, for in due time it shall return back to dust, from which it came. Be concerned about strengthening your spirit; it will last through eternity. For what cannot be seen is more important than what can be seen. We will only experience life eternal through Jesus. It's important to die to self daily so that you decrease and allow God to increase in every area of your life. When we die to self, we begin to experience a new life through Christ. Don't just exist. Live a life that is pleasing to God.

NOTES:

June 13
A Gradual Change

2 Peter 3:9 (NLT)

God is extremely patient with us. This is due to the fact that he's a loving and forgiving God. He does not ask that you have it all together. In fact, he'll meet you right where you are and change your heart over time. God knows what you struggle with, what you aren't ready to give up, where your focus is right now, why you feel the way you do and how to bring you closer to him. All you need to do is be a willing vessel. Be willing to walk in the light of God. Allow God to shape and mold you into who he wants you to be. It will be a gradual change. God has patience with you, so have patience while God is working on you.

NOTES:

June 14
Holiness And Purity

2 Peter 3:14 (NLT)

While you wait for what God has in store for you, don't stop doing good. Everything that is good is not popular. Yet, God has called you to walk in holiness and purity. You will at times fall short of these efforts, but God sees that you're trying. It's important to spend time with God daily so that you know what he has called you to do. The things he has called you to do might not be what you see on television, what you hear on the radio or even what you are frequent in doing. It will be something fresh, something new and something great, because he's doing a new work within you. If you stay faithful unto death, you will reap the harvest God has just for you.

NOTES:

June 15
Grateful

Isaiah 9:6 (ESV)

Thank God for Jesus. Thank God for sending his only begotten son to die for you. Thank God that through the shed blood of Jesus dying on the cross, that you receive freedom. There is no one you know, walking this earth, that would endure what Jesus did for you. There is no love like the love that God showed, when he sent his son to die for you, that you may inherit eternal life. Don't allow what Jesus did to be in vain. Live your life according to the commands from God; do what is pleasing in the sight of the Lord and praise God always.

NOTES:

June 16
Never Let Your Light Dim

2 Corinthians 4:7 (NLT)

The light that you represent on earth is God. The love that you show others is from God. When people see you, they should see the light and love that is Christ Jesus. The more time spent in prayer and reading his Word, the brighter your light will shine. If you've allowed your light to dim, do what you need to do to get it back shining brightly. There are dark places in this world that need your presence. When you step on the scene you change the atmosphere. Don't be afraid of the calling on your life, God has a purpose and plan for you. Allow God's light to shine through you daily.

NOTES:

June 17
Jesus Christ Is Our Greatest Example

Philippians 2:6-7 (NLT)

The greatest example for us to follow is Jesus Christ. God actually sent Jesus so that we would follow in the greatness thereof. Jesus shows us what the outcome of obedience is. Jesus shows us what being a willing vessel truly is. Jesus shows us how to endure persecution. Jesus shows us how to love everyone, despite what they may do. Jesus shows us what true friendship is. Jesus shows us why living for God is essential. Jesus shows us that it's not about us. Jesus shows us why we were chosen by God. Ask God to renew your mind, body and spirit so that you can walk in the greatness God has called you to, by being an example of Christ on the earth.

NOTES:

June 18
All For You

2 Corinthians 8:9 (ESV)

What Jesus endured on earth was all for you. Knowing that although he was rich, he became poor, and through his poverty you might become rich. Never take for granted what Jesus did for you. Through Jesus, your life is enriched and full of purpose. Jesus came that you may experience the goodness that God has laid out for you. You have a God that loves you unconditionally, completely accepts you, totally forgives you and values you more than you value yourself. You are blessed, to be a blessing.

NOTES:

June 19
Take The Limits Off

Romans 8:32 (NIV)

There is no limit to what God can do for you. When you put a limit on what you think God can do for you, you limit yourself. God can do far above anything that you can ask or think. He holds all power in his hands. Everything that you ever thought of or imagined, God created that thing. Expect God to move on your behalf in a miraculous way. The longer you try to keep God in a box, the longer it will take for you to see results. God is ready to move miraculously in you, through you and around you. As soon as you take the limits off God, you will see his blessings and anointing over your life flow freely. Take God out of that box that you have him in.

NOTES:

June 20
Encounter God Daily

1 Timothy 6:15-16 (NLT)

Every day should be a day that you have an encounter with the Holy Spirit, times where you experience God on a supernatural level. During this time God will reveal himself to you, he will give you commands, he will renew your spirit and give you confirmation. When you hear God tell you to set some time aside for him, do it. Be disciplined and obedient to the things that God has called you to. You may not understand it now but it will be revealed to you when God feels you're ready. The longer you walk in disobedience of what you know God is speaking to you, the longer you will be in the place you're in. God is not hiding anything from you; be obedient to his Word and his plans for your life will be revealed to you.

NOTES:

June 21
Worthy Of Your Praise

Psalm 92:1-5 (NLT)

A sure way for God to know that you appreciate everything that he's doing for you, is to give him praise and glory. Not only for what he's done but just for who he is. God has been amazing to you. No matter your circumstances, no matter your situation, no matter what you've faced in life or what you will endure in the future, God is worthy to be praised. Even if God never blesses you again, you have so much to be thankful for. Think on where God has brought you from and where he is taking you. You have so much to be thankful for. God never takes a break and never gets tired—what an awesome God we serve. You owe God everything. Today, praise him with everything in you.

NOTES: Papa, may it never be about the blessings but about you - the Blesser. Thank you for all that you are. I'm sorry for putting the things of this world before you - both material possessions or even social media or TV. I want to give you first place in my life. I thank you & love you. Thank you for loving me

June 22
Listen

Isaiah 50:4 (GNT)

Those who have an ear let them hear. God is speaking to his children and is giving commands for you to follow daily. God wants you to go out and be light in this dark world. Every day, God puts something in your belly to speak to his people. You may not recognize it until it happens, but it's happening. Anything that leads people to the light and love of Christ is from God. Wherever God positions you, do the will of God to the best of your ability, remembering always that God will use any willing vessel to bring souls to his kingdom. Don't allow fear to stop you from doing the will of your Father.

NOTES: Thank you Papa, for the boldness to share what you've placed within me to bring glory & honor to your name. There is so much in me that you want to use but I keep getting myself in the way. Show me. Lead me. Guide me by the power of your Holy Spirit, I need to remind myself consistently that you are the potter and I am merely the clay.

June 23
Just Believe

Hebrews 11:1 (ESV)

Faith is having confidence that God can and will do what you've asked him to do. God has it under control, so don't lose hope. God can do the impossible, so don't stop believing. Expect God to move in miraculous ways on your behalf. Everything that you hope for and dream about can and will take place if you believe. There are no limits to what God can do in your life. God has already proven to you that he will take care of you, that he loves you and that he will never leave or forsake you. Your position now should be to expect God to move and to praise him until it comes to fruition. God's timing is perfect, so if it hasn't taken place yet, he's preparing you for the greatness ahead.

NOTES:

And if not, He is still good.

2021

June 24
The Will Of Your Heavenly Father

Galatians 1:10 (ESV)

When you try to win the approval of people, you are not doing the will of your Father. Seek rather to do the will of your Father who has ordained you for a purpose. God has called you and set you apart. The only approval you need is from God. You can miss what God has for you when you seek the approval of people, because this takes your focus away from what God has called you to do. You can't do the will of people and do the will of God at the same time. God wants you to be free today of human expectations. There is a calling on your life, and in order to fully walk in it you need to seek God with your whole heart.

NOTES:

I cannot do the will of God and do the will of people at the same time. He has set me apart.

June 25
Know God's Word For Yourself

Galatians 1:9 (ESV)

It's essential to know the Word of God for yourself, to hide the Word in your heart so that it does not depart from you. For in the coming days there will be those preaching the gospel, contrary to what you've learned and studied. Don't be swayed by the false prophets that are coming, God will deal with them according to his will. You shall stand firm on the Word of God that you know to be true. Be faithful unto death and you will surely inherit eternal life through Christ Jesus your Lord.

NOTES:

June 26
True Conversion

Act 4:18-20 (NLT)

When you know for yourself that God is real, you can't help but share him with everyone you know. It's not until you experience a true conversion that you know that God is real. You begin to see things that once weren't as visible, you begin to hear things that once weren't as audible, you begin to feel his presence that once wasn't reachable and you begin to have a teachable spirit that receives things that you weren't so open to. When God works through you, miracles happen.

NOTES:

June 27
God Has Total Control

DECLARE!

Isaiah 41:10 (ESV)

God has everything under control. Have faith in God! Believing always that he can make a way out of no way. Fear did not come from God. Being discouraged did not come from God. Feeling burdened did not come from God. Feeling unworthy did not come from God. Having suicidal thoughts did not come from God. Don't allow Satan and his tactics to overwhelm you, burden you or take control of you. Take back everything that the devil has stolen from you. Declare today that you will have peace, declare that you will experience joy, declare that you are the head and not the tail, declare that you are worthy, declare that you will live and not die, declare that you are free and declare that you have a sound mind. Your life has purpose and God thinks so highly of you. So don't accept what the devil tries to plant in your mind. You shall win the battle.

NOTES:

June 28
But God

James 1:2-4 (ESV)

You have been equipped by God to endure everything that is placed before you. Everything might not make sense and you may not enjoy it all. But God! Thank God for allowing you to endure through your trials. Thank God for the tests that come your way. Thank God for not making it easy. For if everything that you endured was easy, you would not rely on God like you do. You would not spend as much time with God like you do. Without having to deal with the things that you deal with, you wouldn't realize how strong you really are. God is building you up for greatness. Everything that you go through is not solely for you. So remember the next time that you go through trials, ask God whom will you be helping by overcoming and enduring the test that has been placed in front of you. This too shall pass. Get ready for your breakthrough.

NOTES:

June 29
A Spiritual War

Ephesians 6:12 (GNT)

There is a war going on. It's a spiritual war, a war in the spirit, not the flesh. Every day you wake up, you need to be ready for battle. Satan doesn't want you happy if you're a child of God. His goal is to steal, kill and destroy you by any means. But God! God sent Jesus to die for us, and his blood covers us when the enemy attacks. If you feel attacked, like you can't catch a break, remember that your battle is in the spirit, not the flesh. The only way to be prepared for a daily battle is through the Word of God and prayer. Allow God to be your strength, allow God to go before you in battle, and make sure that you have your full armor on, at all times.

NOTES:

June 30
Unconditional Love

Psalm 89:15-16 (NIV)

We serve an awesome God. It should be a goal of yours to fall in love daily with Jesus. Build a lifelong relationship with your creator, not just a religious experience. As you spend time with God you will feel his presence, you will hear his voice with clarity and you will gain understanding of the will he has for your life. God will reveal to you all of who he is, his plans for your life and answers to the questions you've asked.

Without the presence of God in your life, you'll find yourself searching for the unknown. With the presence of God, you'll experience peace, joy and blessings in abundance. Draw close to God and God will draw close to you.

NOTES:

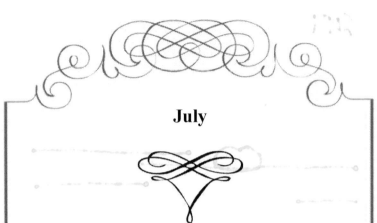

July

"And without faith it is impossible to please him, for whoever would draw near to God must believe that he exists and that he rewards those who seek him."

—Hebrews 11:6 (ESV)

Everlasting Help

Psalm 46:1 (NIV)

God wants to be your strength in times of trouble, in times of despair, in times of doubt, during times you're overwhelmed and during times that you feel burdened.

Will you allow God to help you? Will you lean on God for strength?

The closer your relationship becomes with God, the more you'll realize he will truly supply all your needs and give you the desires of your heart. God has never left you, nor forsaken you. God has never stopped loving you and he continues to bless you daily. Stay focused on God's promise; spend more time with him daily; don't be so hard on yourself, and realize that your help comes from God. Receive your strength today from the Lord, in Jesus' name.

NOTES:

Stay:
Focused on God's promises
Spend more time with Him
Don't be so hard on myself
Realize that my help comes
from God

Hebrews 13:15 (ESV)

There should be praise on your lips, toward God every second of every day. Praise for who God is. Praise for what God has done. Praise for making provisions for your life. Praise for your safety. Praise for your life. Praise for your family. Praise for your friends.

Praise for your ministerial assignment. Praise for your trials. Praise for your triumphs. Praise for your tests. Praise for your blessings. Praise for making a way out of no way. Praise for choosing you. Praise for getting you through. Praise for not giving up on you. Praise for forgiving you. Praise for seeing beyond your faults. Praise for your breakthrough. Praise the name of the Lord, for he is worthy to be praised!

NOTES:

July 3
A Thankful Heart

Ephesians 2:8-9 (ESV)

God's grace is sufficient. Take a second to realize some things. First, think of every sin that you commit daily and how you can ask for forgiveness and it is forgiven. Second, think of all the times that you stepped away from the faith or took a break. Now realize who was always there with open arms to welcome you back. Third, think about all the people who've disappointed you in life, who've harmed you, put dirt on your name and tried to cause confusion. Now think of how God turned those situations around and helped you see the positive in it. God is the one who gives you peace through the storm, whose love is everlasting, whose protection is covering you, whose grace is sufficient, who holds the higher power, who can transform any negative situation into positive. We don't give God enough praise. Today, just thank him for his grace by faith.

NOTES:

2021

July 4
Be Thankful

Philippians 4:6-7 (ESV)

Will you be content with what you have? If you have little or if you have much, God is still God. God will make sure that all your needs are met. There is (nothing) in this world that God can't do for you. He can do anything

Are you thankful in the space that God has you in right now?

For in a blink of an eye God can change situations, circumstances, finances, relationships, friendships, health issues, etc. Do not be anxious about anything, but in every situation by prayer and petition, with thanksgiving, present your requests to God. Trust that God hears your request, lean not on your own understanding, but allow God to direct your path. Remember, God is still God no matter what the situation looks like.

And if not, He is still good!

NOTES:

July 5
My Inheritance

Ephesians 1:18-20 (GNT)

There is an inheritance in heaven that God promises all of his children. Your inheritance is above anything that you could ever ask or think. We, his children, have to continue on this faith walk to get to our inheritance. It's not about what worldly possessions you can stack up while you're living on earth, because you can't take that with you. It's about the relationship with your Father, it's about winning souls to his Kingdom, and it's about loving God and loving his people. You received the free gift of salvation the moment you accepted Jesus Christ as Lord of your life. The road may be rocky, the valley may seem deep and the struggle may seem too hard to get through. But God! God makes your inheritance worth it. Everything that you're going through is a part of God's plan for you. Stay focused and continue to strive for greatness.

NOTES:

July 6
Seek God With Expectancy

Psalm 105:4 (ESV)

When you seek God with all of your heart, you are guaranteed to find him. God is forever present wherever you are. There is nowhere you can go to hide from him. If you want a stronger relationship with God, seek him daily. If you want to hear God speaking directly to you, seek him in prayer. If you want peace in your life, seek the peace of God. If you need strength right now, seek God in your weakness. If you have a desire to be disciplined in what God has called you to, seek God in your obedience. Seek God first and all things shall be added to you. Don't doubt what God can do, seek him and you will find him, when you seek him with all your heart.

NOTES:
" If you have a desire to

July 7
Stand Against The Enemy

Jude 1:24-25 (ESV)

There are stumbling blocks that are set before you daily by the enemy. You have a choice to trip over them or step over them. Remember that you became a target for the enemy the moment that you gave your life to Christ Jesus. There are tricks, tactics and schemes that are thrown at you by the enemy. Connecting with God daily will allow you to see these things in the spirit realm. God will make you aware and help you not to stumble or fall. The enemy is laying low, to catch you off guard. This is why spending time with God is so essential. The more time you spend with God, the more equipped you will be, to stand against the tactics of the enemy.

NOTES:

July 8
Confidence

1 John 3:19-20 (NIV)

The fact that God knows everything and you are his child should give you confidence. Confidence in knowing that he hides nothing from his children. Avail yourself to the Lord and he will lift you up. Be willing and obedient and you shall receive every great thing that God has ordained for your life. Allow your life to glorify God like never before. Don't dwell on your past. God will forgive and forget everything you've done that is not like him. From this day forward, make a commitment to stay disciplined and obedient in what he has called you to do. You will then begin to see God's plan for your life unfold. Walk in the purpose that God has for you.

NOTES:

July 9
Reverence To Our Heavenly Father

Psalm 29:2 (NLT)

How often do you worship God just for who he is?

Many times we go to God for what we need or desire. We go to God when we are in a bind. We go to God when things are at its worst and we don't know where to turn. We go to God when things aren't looking good, on our behalf. We go to God when we feel lost. We go to God when we feel alone and unworthy. We go to God when we think no one else will understand us.

How often do you go to God just to praise his holy name?

God commands us to worship his name. There is a sweet peace when you praise the name of the Lord. Don't get so caught up in yourself that you forget to worship and praise God. Try not asking God for anything today; make today all about God. Bask in the presence of God, expressing to him how much he means to you, expressing how much you love and adore him. God deserves all your praise and worship. Make it your daily priority to give God the glory and honor that is due his name.

NOTES:

Psalm 116:5-7 (GNT)

There is new mercy bestowed on you each day. God has brought you from a mighty long way. Who you were and who you are today, God made that transformation possible. Through his grace, he was patient with you. Through his grace he has forgiven the many sins you've committed. Through grace, God has shown you that your life matters to him. Through grace God proves to you that he hears you and that he works miracles on your behalf. God sees the potential in all your flaws. God knows your struggles and will help you break free of them. God hears your pleas for help and is there to rescue you. There is no one more merciful than the God we serve. His grace is sufficient.

NOTES:

July 11
Have A Thankful Heart

Ephesians 5:20 (GNT)

Allow God to create a thankful heart within you. There are plenty of things that you should be thankful for. Don't overlook the things that seem small, because tomorrow you might wake up in lack of that very thing that you took for granted. Take time daily to communicate with God that you are thankful for all that he has done, all that he's doing and all that he will do. Take your eyes off your problems and look toward heaven with the spiritual eyes of Christ. For every moment that you're complaining, that's a stolen moment from giving God praise in your thankfulness. Expressing your thankfulness to God shows that you love and appreciate who he is.

NOTES:

2021

1 Corinthians 6:19 (ESV)

You did not create yourself. Therefore, you do not know what's best for you. You do not belong to yourself. Therefore, stop trying to run your own life. You see, you need God. He's the creator of all things, including you. You need the direction of the Holy Spirit daily. If you do not have direction from the Holy Spirit, whomever is leading you is leading you astray. With God you'll be led straight to your destiny. Following anyone but Christ Jesus will only lead you to destruction. Being a child of God leads to greatness; you've been called and chosen by God to do his will. Walk in the light of Christ.

NOTES:

July 13
Your Spirit Needs Substance

John 7:38-39 (ESV)

To experience God on a supernatural level means to experience the Holy Spirit and its gifts. Once you realize that you can get high off the spirit of God, you will long for his presence like never before. You will thirst after the living water that only comes through the Holy Spirit. Our natural bodies are filled with a spirit that needs substance. Never allow your spirit to get dehydrated or to go hungry. Your life will reflect what you feed your spirit, on a daily basis. If you choose to live life in abundance, do what it is that God has called you to do in the spirit.

NOTES:

July 14
Be Transparent

Psalm 139:23-24 (GNT)

Allow God to search your heart daily. This means that you show God everything about you. Don't try and hide anything; God knows all things anyway. Pour out your heart to God. Ask God to remove anything that is not like him. Ask God to remove burdens, hurt, pain, unworthiness, depression, bitterness and strife. God wants to do a new work within you. Allow God to bring restoration to your life by fully allowing him to search all that you truly are. God can transform your heart and make you whole again. Expect God to do a new work within you when you totally surrender to his will and his ways.

NOTES:

July 15
God Notices Everything

1 Peter 5:6 (ESV)

God notices everything that you commit yourself to. God knows how much effort is being put into the things he has called you to do. Don't worry about receiving accolades for the things that you're doing in life, other people may never notice. But God! God searches the heart and knows if your motives are pure. In due season God will lift you up. So don't be so concerned about what everyone thinks, but be concerned about what God thinks of you. If you remain humble and glorify God with your life, God will set you apart. God will begin to use you in ways you didn't think were possible. Allow God to promote you, and thank God for the harvest that is on the way.

NOTES:

July 16
Be A Good Steward

Job 1:21 (NIV)

The Lord gives and the Lord takes away. Be a good steward over what God gives you. As easily as you received it, it can be as easily taken away. You came into this world with nothing and you shall leave here just the same. So don't get so wrapped up in all of the material things and lose focus on what God has placed you here for. There are tons of things to possess in this world, yet none of them compare to what you will possess in eternity. Have an attitude of gratitude while you're serving God on this earth. Before you know it, you'll begin your life in eternity and live with no concern for worldly possessions.

NOTES:

July 17
Sweet Rest

Exodus 33:14 (NIV)

In the presence of the Lord you will find sweet rest. Daily you should make it a point to get in the presence of God. Spending alone time with God is an assurance that you will receive rest in his presence. There is no reason that you should go a day without experiencing God's love, joy and peace on a consistent basis. God wants you to take a step back from the cares of life and saturate yourself in his presence. Everything that you're searching for can be found when you spend alone time with God. Let today be the beginning of a new start in your life. Experience God on a supernatural level today. Cast your cares on him and bask in the sweet rest he bestows on you today.

NOTES:

July 18
Give Honor Where It's Due

Galatians 6:7 (NIV)

Do everything to honor God and not man. Each day God gives you an assignment, this assignment is to bring glory to the name of the Lord. When you know your daily assignment, you'll realize that it's not about you, but it's about how God will work through you. When you're a willing vessel, God will use you in ways that seem impossible to man. There is nothing that God can't accomplish through you. You just have to keep your eyes focused on Jesus, trust his timing, be patient and always give him the praise that is due his name. Your destiny has everything to do with the way you allow God to use you for his glory. Trust God through the process and remain humble when God begins to move on your behalf.

NOTES:

Psalm 16:8 (NIV)

God wants to do something supernatural in you and through you. Remove that spirit of fear from your mind right now. Remove that spirit of doubt from your mind right now. Remove that spirit of unworthiness from your mind right now. You shall stand in the midst of adversity and not be moved. You shall stand in the midst of trials and not be shaken. When you rely totally on God, he will use you in ways that you sometimes won't understand. No matter what you face in life, stand firm on the Word of God, for he is always with you. God will turn adversity into something supernatural. God will turn your trials into triumphs. God will turn your cries into pure joy. Stay faithful unto death and you will receive the gift of eternal life.

NOTES:

July 20
Love Is Eternal

Romans 8:38-39 (ESV)

God's love for you is eternal. There is nothing that you can do, that can separate you from the love that God has for you. When you turn your back on God, he still showers you with love. When you put God on a shelf, he still loves you. When you sin against God, his love is still shown to you. When you go days without talking to God, he still loves you. When you aren't obedient to God, he still loves you. God's love is not based on how you treat him. God's love is not based on stuff and things. God's love is not based on accolades or gifts. God has loved you since before creation and he will continue to love you through our eternity. God loves you more than you love yourself. Nothing can measure up to the way God loves you. Today, find confidence knowing that God's love for you endures forever. From this day forward, never question the love God has for you.

NOTES:

July 21
Fear God Only

Luke 12:5 (ESV)

There is no one in the heavenly realm or on earth to fear but God alone. Don't fear people and certainly don't fear Satan. For people can only do things to your physical body, which will eventually return to dust from which it came. The enemy only has the authority given to him by God, and you have the choice each day not to take the bait. Fear God, knowing that he has the authority to cast you into hell or allow you to reign in the heavenly realm. Your life resides in God's hands. Your plans for the rest of your life ultimately sit with God and will only manifest, if God allows them to. So yes, fear the one true living God that makes all things come to pass.

NOTES:

July 22
Authenticity

Luke 12:8 (ESV)

Be an authentic example of Christ on the earth. Someone is watching you and wants to have a real relationship with Christ because of you. Don't be afraid to share your walk with Christ, and acknowledge him in all that you do. The reason God has taken you through the things that you've been through is so you can show people how real God truly is. If you didn't go through things, some people would never know how God truly works. But because you've been through and got through, they know that God is real. Don't be ashamed of where you've been. Be thankful that God has you in the space that he has you in now. Your trials made you stronger. Your tests helped strengthen you. Your triumphs gave you courage to press on. Your teachable spirit allows you to trust God, walk by faith and endure, despite what is going on around you. Continue to profess the name of the Lord and don't be ashamed of being a child of God.

NOTES:

July 23
Allow Your Spirit To Be In Control

Galatians 5:16 (NLT)

Stop allowing the desires of your flesh to rule your life. You have total control over your flesh and the desires thereof. It's essential to allow your spirit to direct your life. When you hide God's Word in your heart it will not depart from you. The Word of God feeds your spirit, and your desires feed your flesh. You have to choose daily whether you will give in to your fleshly desires or if your spirit will take total control. When your spirit is nourished and it's not dehydrated, you have a better chance in walking in the spirit instead of the flesh. God's will for your life is that you do the will of your Father. This means that you should tap into the spirit of God daily to draw strength from him. If the spirit of God is not ruling your life, you are being led to destruction. Do the will of your Father and allow God's spirit to reign supreme in your life from this day forward.

NOTES:

July 24
God's Favor

Exodus 33:13 (NLT)

You shall find favor in the sight of the Lord when you walk in obedience to him. God's plans are not your plans, nor his ways your ways. When what you want out of life aligns with God's will for your life, you will begin to see those things manifest. The favor of the Lord is upon your life today. What you've been praying for will come to pass. What you've been waiting for will soon come to fruition. Those dreams God has placed in your belly are in the works. When you trust in the Lord with all your heart and lean not on your own understanding, you will begin to see miracles take place in your life. God wants to do something new in you. When you are obedient to the Word of God, you will recognize the favor of the Lord over your life now and forever more. Look out for the miraculous works happening all around you. God is an amazing God.

NOTES:

July 25
Total Surrender

Psalm 139:23-24 (ESV)

Allow God to examine you from the inside out. When you surrender totally to God that allows him to work fully through you. Stop trying to hide those things that you are battling internally, God sees them. Allow God to take out everything in you that is not like him. Be willing to release yourself of the things that do not please God even if they feel good to the flesh. If God asks you to release it, let it go. When you do what God has asked of you, you will see him do the things that you've asked of him. It's time to clean out everything that is within you that is not like God, so that he can replace it with everything that is like him. Ask God to renew your mind, renew your body and renew your spirit. God is ready to do a new work within you; be willing to receive everything that he has for you.

NOTES:

July 26
God Thinks Highly Of You

Psalm 139:17-18 (NIV)

God thinks highly of you, and his thoughts of you are all precious. There are numerous things that God says about you that you may not think of yourself. You are worthy. You are the head and not the tail. You are the lender and not the borrower. You are above and not beneath. You are special to God. You are unique. You are talented. You are a part of a royal priesthood. You are loved. You are adored. You are amazing in God's eyes. You were created with a purpose. You are a blessing to God. The list of all the wonderful thoughts that God has about you cannot be numbered. Remember that God created you in his image, and everything that he created is good. God loves and adores you, and your life is full of purpose. Live in the confidence of knowing that God thinks highly of you.

NOTES:

July 27
God Is With You

John 15:20 (NIV)

Don't be surprised by what you will endure during your lifetime. For what you will endure is nothing compared to what Jesus endured in his life on earth. Jesus warns us that if people persecuted him, they will surely do it to you because you are his disciple. The promise from our father is that he will always be with us. Whether you are being persecuted for the teaching of Jesus or you are giving a rhema word to his people, the Holy Spirit is with you. Don't stop doing good on account of what you're going through. Receive clarity from the Holy Spirit about what you will endure and why, and walk in the purpose God destined for you. God is able to do exceedingly above all that you can ask or think.

NOTES:

July 28
In The World, Not Of The World

John 15:18-19 (ESV)

You do not belong to the world. You are in this world but not of this world. For what Christ has for your life far exceeds what this world can offer you. The tangible things that this world has to offer will soon pass away. You may wonder why there aren't more people who seek after God's Word and actually pursue it. This is because the world hates what Jesus stands for. If they hate what Jesus stands for, they hate you because you follow Christ's teachings. Find confidence while you walk in the spirit and not the flesh. The Holy Spirit will strengthen you during your journey on this earth. Everyone won't believe in what you stand for, but keep standing. Everyone won't fight in the spirit for what they believe in, but never give up. We serve a God that will give you strength to endure. Strive for greatness.

NOTES:

July 29
Nothing Hidden

John 15:15 (ESV)

There is nothing that Jesus hides from you. Things may come as a surprise to you, but they are not hidden from you. When you seek the face of the Lord he will begin to reveal to you his plans for your life and the promises that he has made to you. The more you seek God, the more your life will align with the will of God. Jesus calls you friend, instead of servant because you know what your master in heaven has in store for you. The Lord gives you daily direction through prayer, the Bible and meditation. Don't slack on spending time with God. This is a sure way that you will be able to be on one accord with God. The greatness that God has in store for you will only be revealed to you when you spend time with him. Today, set aside time just to bask in the presence of the Lord.

NOTES:

John 15:12 (ESV)

Jesus has called you to love everybody. There are no stipulations to which you are to love. God says to love everybody. This can be a hard task when you don't understand why God has called you to love. You have been called to love everybody because God is love, and you can't represent God on the earth if you are opposed to loving everyone. Love sees no face. Love sees no race. Love sees no religion. Love sees no educational background. Love sees no status. Love sees no right or wrong. Love sees no flaw. Love sees spirit. Love sees a need. Love sees beyond fault. Love sees beyond guilt. Love finds good in every situation. Love is God. To know love is to know God, because God is love.

NOTES:

July 31
Win Souls

John 15:1-2 (NIV)

God has assigned individuals for you to win to his kingdom. When you win these individuals, you are bearing good fruit. Somebody somewhere is waiting to hear your testimony. Somebody somewhere is going through the storm you just came out of. Somebody somewhere is not opening a Bible but is watching you and hanging on to your very words. These individuals that are assigned to you can only go as far as you go. Do what God has called you to do in order to effectively lead the sheep that he has allowed you to shepherd. Someone is always watching you; learn to be a great example of Jesus on the earth.

NOTES:

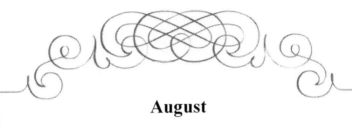

August

"Everything you do, O God, is holy. No god is as great as you. You are the God who works miracles; you showed your might among the nations."

—Psalm 77:13-14 (GNT)

August 1
Love Like Jesus Loves

Matthew 5:43-44 (ESV)

A great example of loving God and loving people is illustrated through the life of Jesus Christ. We are called to love everybody. Not just those who are worthy of our love, but those who aren't as well. Think of how unworthy you are of the love of God because you sin against him daily. The same way you are loved despite what you've done is the same way God wants you to love everybody. This only becomes a hard task if you make it a hard task. Loving others would come rather easy if you allowed the Holy Spirit to guide you. What you can't do, God can.

God is able to renew your heart; God is able to give you a new way of thinking; God is able to help you forgive; God is able to lead you in the way that you should go; God is able to help you love the unlovable and do good to those who hurt you. God is able to do exceedingly above all you ask or think. Walk in love today, knowing that you were called to share God's love with everybody.

NOTES:

August 2
Your Obedience Is Important

Matthew 5:19 (NIV)

The commands given by God are very crucial to your walk. These are written rules that must be followed. In your obedience to these commands from God you will begin to see God's hand in everything. It is critical that you take what God has spoken to you and apply it to your life. In doing that, you will draw men and women to the light of Christ. Be careful not to lead anyone away from the Word of God by justifying your actions or twisting the Word of God to meet your lifestyle. God will surely judge you for that. Ask God for an appetite for his Word, a willing heart to obey and ears that hear with clarity. God is ready to take you to the new heights, in him.

NOTES:

August 3
A Pure Heart

Matthew 5:8 (NIV)

In order to get to the place that God has called you to, your heart needs to be pure. This means that you have to get rid of some things and let go of some things in order to fully walk in the purpose God has for you. You will be blessed when you release to God all that is burdening you. You will be blessed when you can forgive those who have done wrong to you. You will be blessed when you learn to love those who seem unlovable. There is a blessing on the other side of forgiveness. There is a blessing on the other side of anger and bitterness. There is a blessing on the other side of your brokenness. Today, ask God to give you a pure heart, and release to God everything that is not like him so that you can walk in the life God has chosen for you.

NOTES:

August 4
Called To Be Great

Matthew 5:6 (NLT)

God has called you to greatness. In order to fully walk in the greatness God has for you, you need to desire to do the things God has called you to. When you are obedient to what God has called you to do, you'll begin to see God work on your behalf in miraculous ways. The more time you spend with God, the greater your appetite for his Word will become. The voice of God will become so clear to you that when you go against His voice you will feel conviction. Get out of the habit of doing things your way; you're leading yourself in circles. Rely on God to guide you in the ways that you should go so that you fully walk in the purpose God has destined for your life.

NOTES:

August 5
Truth Is God's Word

John 8:32 (ESV)

The truth of the Lord shall set you free. God wants you to know that you can always rely on his Word. The Bible is the true guide for all those who want to live in the glory of God through eternity. There is nothing that you can find in the Word of God that is not true. Walk in confidence knowing that if you are living according to God's Word, you are living the truth. No matter who goes against it, no matter who tells you that what you believe is wrong, no matter who doesn't believe in the God that you serve, God's Word will manifest itself, and the truth shall set you free. God is the truth, and whoever walks in the ways of the Lord, walks in truth.

NOTES:

August 6
Strive For Greatness

Galatians 4:9 (ESV)

You have known how great of an experience it has been to live for Jesus Christ. Satan would want you to go back to your old ways of doing things, but don't take the bait. What God has to offer you is so much greater than what the world has to offer. You were once living for yourself, now is the time to live for God. It doesn't matter if you occasionally slip up; God knows we have a sinful nature. The goal is to continue to strive for greatness, never to return to the old you that died once you gave your life to Christ. You are a new creature through Christ Jesus. Walk in the greatness that God has for you.

NOTES:

August 7
Let God Lead

Galatians 4:8 (ESV)

It's time to recognize where you've been and where God is trying to take you. You were once enslaved to the world, the world and the things of the world were your god. But now that you've given your life to Christ, you are no longer in slavery. Your freedom was paid for by the price of the blood of Jesus Christ, and you can now walk into your destiny. The plan that God has for you has everything to do with loving God and loving his people. You shall do great things on the earth—expect it and walk in it. Don't allow others to hang your past over your head; you are no longer that person. Walk in boldness with confidence, knowing that God is doing a new work in you and through you.

NOTES:

August 8
Your Inheritance

Galatians 4:6-7 (ESV)

There is an inheritance with your name on it, waiting for you. You are an heir to the throne of God, just like Jesus. You are no longer a slave. You are a son or daughter in Christ. This means that all that God has stored up for you will come to pass. Every promise that is in the Word of God shall come to pass. What the world offers you cannot compare to what God has in store for you, as heir to his throne. There is a place in the heavenly realm with your name on it. Your inheritance excels beyond anything you can think or imagine. Make sure that your life aligns with God's will so that you inherit all that God has for you.

NOTES:

August 9
Free Will

Psalm 4:6-8 (GNT)

God is still God, no matter what is going on around you. Whether you are experiencing the worst times in your life right now or the best times in your life, God will give you peace. Everything that is happening to you right now is not to be blamed on God. Things are happening based on your actions and your choices. Learn not to blame God for what you got yourself into; God gives you free will. Better days will come when you actually sit and listen to the commands of God and obey them. If God has not shown you what to do next, don't move on it according to what you think. It's crucial to spend time with God daily so that you are being led in the ways that you should go. Never depart from the Word of God.

NOTES:

August 10
The Light Of The World

Revelation 21:23 (GNT)

God is the light of the world. Without God there would only be darkness. Even if the sun never shone or the moon did not brighten the night, God's light would illuminate the world. It's important that we shine our light wherever we go, as we are being an example of Christ on the earth. When you step on the scene your light should change the atmosphere. When you step on the scene your light should expel darkness. Your light attracts individuals to you, which in turn attracts individuals to Jesus Christ. It's imperative that you seek God regularly, that you pray without ceasing, that you stay in the Word of God and that you fellowship with like-minded believers so that your light will continue to be fueled.

NOTES:

August 11
Guidance

Luke 12:10 (ESV)

God sent the Holy Spirit to lead and guide you while you live on this earth. It is critical to listen to the things that the Holy Spirit shares with you. These are instructions from God to lead and guide you in the ways that you should go so that what God wants for you in this life is made clear to you. There will be times that you don't quite understand what is being relayed to you, there will be times when you don't want to do what you're commanded to do and there will be times when you want answers but the Holy Spirit is silent. During these times never speak against the Holy Spirit; this you will not be forgiven for. Learn to trust God wholeheartedly, have a teachable spirit and stay encouraged.

NOTES:

August 12
More Than Stuff And Things

Luke 12:15 (ESV)

A true fact is that no matter how much you store up on earth, these things will not make it to heaven with you. God encourages you to guard yourself from all covetousness, for you shall take nothing with you. The riches in this world can't compare to the riches in heaven. Take your eyes off your possessions and keep your eyes focused on the one who gives you everything in abundance. Don't get to a point where what you have makes you or breaks you. If you're living only to inherit stuff and things, you aren't living at all. God has created worldly possessions for your enjoyment, but your true life is not made up of stuff and things. Your true self is made up of Spirit, which will inherit eternal life without material possessions or a fleshly body.

NOTES:

August 13
More Than What The Eye Can See

Luke 12:22-23 (NIV)

What God created you for is much more than how you look, how you smell, how good your hair looks, how flawless your makeup is, how cute you look in your designer clothes, how big your house is, how nice your car is, how big your bank account is, etc. God created your spirit first and placed your spirit into a fleshly body. Be more concerned about your spirit than what your physical body portrays. God knows you from the inside out, and he is well pleased when your spirit is nourished. Don't be so caught up on looks, fashion, fast cars, money and houses that you miss the most important aspect of your being, which is spirit. You are much more than how you look and how you dress; God birthed your spirit to reach lives for his kingdom.

NOTES:

August 14
Live, Don't Just Exist

Luke 12:25-26 (NIV)

Live in the moment, for tomorrow shall take care of itself. God did not create you to worry or to be anxious for what is to come. God wants you to live instead of just existing in this world today. There is a surprise waiting for you each day, and because you actually never know what it is until it is given to you, enjoy the gift God gives you daily. The best way to enjoy the gift of today is to only focus on what is happening today. You don't have to live in the past; the past should not hinder you right now. You don't know what the future holds, yet you prepare for it like you are the creator of it. Today, learn to bask in the gift of life. Don't worry about tomorrow, for it shall take care of itself.

NOTES:

August 15
Much Required Of You

Luke 12:48 (ESV)

There are requirements set by God to achieve greatness. If you want to be great in the Kingdom of God, there are many things that will be required of you. In return, God will give you the desires of your heart. Don't ever expect to receive something for nothing. God gives you commands to follow each day; from this your obedience is tested. Whatever God has entrusted you with, whether it be people, places or things, God requires something even greater from you than what you were entrusted with. Get ready for what God has in store for you. Be ready to take responsibility for what God will entrust you with and watch God use you in a mighty way.

NOTES:

August 16
Strength

Philippians 4:13 (NLT)

You can do all things through Christ who gives you strength. When you are feeling weak, surrender to God and allow him to fill you with strength. When you're feeling tired, remember that calling on the name of the Lord will give you strength. When you want to throw in the towel, remember that your push to keep going forward comes from the Lord. When you're down and out, remember that you are not counted out because your strength comes from the Lord. All things are possible if first you believe. God has greatness in store for you and he will strengthen you daily, in your walk, if you trust in him and allow him to build you up daily. God knows the end at the beginning, and he has sent the Holy Spirit to help you get through each day.

NOTES:

August 17
The Great Creation

Genesis 1:1 (NLT)

Everything that God created is good. From the beginning of time, God created things for his good and nothing was meant for evil. God created you in his image and in his likeness. This means that you were created for his good. It's time to recognize the creation of the world and all the greatness that God has in store for those who earnestly seek after him. For there is nothing that God has created out of formality—you included. God used his precious time to create everything that is in and of the world. Use your precious time wisely while you're on this earth. You were created for a purpose and everything that God has in store for you is good.

NOTES:

August 18
A Leader Of Leaders

Matthew 28:19 (NLT)

There are individuals in your life that will follow you wherever you may go. If this is true, you're a leader. You may not think of yourself as a leader, but that's exactly who you are. God wants you to help build his kingdom with your leadership and to build up disciples for his kingdom. There are individuals that are looking up to you, following you and who want to be just like you. This is why it is crucial to stay in your word, to build an authentic relationship with Christ daily and to pray without ceasing. Individuals that you are leading are not only watching you but they are reading you and mimicking you. Be the best you that God created you to be.

NOTES:

Romans 12:1 (NIV)

There is a sense of peace that overcomes you when you dedicate your body and your life as a living sacrifice to God. This means that you not only stop doing things your way, but you actually begin to serve God with your whole heart, mind and spirit. You will begin to notice that the things you formally desire, you no longer do. You will begin to notice the way you talk and the way you walk actually align with the word of God. You will notice a difference in yourself and others will see it too. You will begin to live for Christ instead of living for yourself and others. Allow God to do a new work in your heart, your mind and your spirit today. Offer yourself as a living sacrifice to God today and allow him to purge you of everything that does not represent him.

NOTES:

August 20
Life According To God's Plan

John 10:10 (ESV)

There is a plan set out for your life. God has a plan for your life and Satan has a plan for your life. You have to choose wisely each day whether to choose God's plan or Satan's plan. There is a distinct difference. God's plan is to give you life in abundance, so everything that is set before you leads you to life everlasting. Everything that is meant to kill, steal or destroy you comes from Satan. These things are sometimes wrapped in something that looks good, smells good and feels good, but you know that it is not good for you. It's your choice. Each day you have to make a choice whether or not to align your life with what God has planned for you or with what Satan has planned for you. Make wise choices from this day forward.

NOTES:

August 21
Speak It

Acts 18:9 (ESV)

There is something that has been birthed inside of you that the devil wants to keep you from speaking. God says, keep on speaking and do not give up. That very thing that God has placed within you will help save lives and be encouragement to someone. No matter how afraid you are and how you think people will perceive you, don't close your mouth. If God has given it to you to speak, speak it and allow the Holy Spirit to work through you. God is ready to use you in miraculous ways, for his glory, to reach the masses. If God instilled it in you, it's just a matter of time until you walk in it. Don't be afraid, what God has in store for you is greater than anything you could ever imagine.

NOTES:

1 John 1:9 (ESV)

God knows that you sin every day, and because of that he wants you to confess your sins daily and ask for forgiveness. When you ask for forgiveness, be sure to also forgive yourself. God keeps no record of wrong; once we ask for forgiveness God forgives us and cleanses us of our unrighteousness. There is no reason for you to hold on to things that God has already forgiven you for. Be free today, repent for your sins and ask God to help you in the areas that you are weak. God is faithful and he will strengthen you where you are weak. Your sins put a wedge between you and God, but repentance brings you back in right standing, with God. There should not be a day that goes by that you don't repent because every day you sin, whether consciously or unconsciously. God is a forgiving God full of grace and mercy; surrender all to him today and allow him to empty you out and fill you with his spirit.

NOTES:

August 23
Sin Is Sin

Romans 3:23 (ESV)

There is no way to measure sin. There is no such thing as a big sin or a little sin, because all sin is sin. This is why God made it clear that we all fall short of his glory. This is to keep us from comparing our sins to one another. We know that we all sin daily and in order to be brought back in right standing with God, we must repent daily. So stop comparing your sins to others to try to justify that your sin is not as big as the next person's sin. God will forgive whomever comes to him with a pure heart and asks for his forgiveness. Forgiveness of sin is not up to you, it's up to God.

NOTES:

August 24
Reverence To God

Romans 14:6 (NLT)

All that you do should be in reverence to God. For God created you for a purpose, and living out that purpose means that you are doing things that are pleasing to God. Your conversations should be pleasing to God. What you do on a daily basis should please God. Where you go daily should be an atmosphere that is pleasing to God. If you know what you do daily does not please God, allow God to change your heart, your mind and your spirit so that you can walk in the purpose God has for you. You will have to let some people go, you will have to let some relationships go, and you will have to let some things go in order for you to eliminate the distractions that Satan has placed in your path. It may be hard at first and it will not happen overnight, but when you are obedient to God you will begin to walk in the greatness God has planned for your life.

NOTES:

August 25
A Teachable Spirit

Matthew 28:20 (NLT)

When you have a teachable spirit you can become a great leader in the Kingdom of God. God wants you to retain everything that he is teaching you in his Word and commanding you in prayer. Once you receive it, share it with others so that they, in return, can share it with others. This is how the Word of the Lord spreads through the earth. If I'm on fire for God and what I'm learning is being applied to my life, those who are following me begin to grasp hold of that and want to share it also. If God is molding and shaping you daily, you will begin to notice it and others will notice it too. It's not just about how much you know, it's about you having the desire to grow. God is doing a new work in you and through you. Allow God to use you like never before.

NOTES:

August 26
Love Unconditional

Romans 5:8 (ESV)

God wants you to know that he really loves you and nothing can separate you from his love. His love for you is so great that he sent his only begotten son to die on the cross for you. His love is so great that no matter what you say or do, his love for you will last through eternity. The times that you feel unloved, God steps in the gap to show you that nothing can separate you from his love. The times that you try to fill voids with stuff, things and people, God steps in and shows you that his love is all that you need. The times that you don't even love yourself, God steps in to show you that through him you are complete. Thank God today that his love for you never fails.

NOTES:

August 27
Daily Guidance

Joshua 1:8 (ESV)

Hide the Word of the Lord in your heart that it will not depart from you. The Bible is your guide for everyday life. It is written for reproof, correction and to train you in righteousness. This is why it is essential to stay in the Word of God and pray without ceasing, because the devil wants to distract you from getting in the face of God daily so that you aren't prosperous and so that you do not succeed in life. The Bible is the law and you need to be in obedience to the law of God. When you are obedient, you will begin to see things work out for your good. There is nothing that God won't do for you. Are you willing to do all that God is asking of you in order to receive the promises that God has for you?

NOTES:

August 28
The Best Gift Is Free

Romans 6:23 (ESV)

There is a free gift of salvation imparted to you when you receive the Son of God, Jesus Christ, as your Lord and Savior. There is a cost for sin, which is death. Because you sin you will die, yet because you are alive through Christ Jesus you will live in eternity, through salvation. There is no price for salvation. No one can take away your salvation once it is given to you. Enjoy the freedom of living this life; knowing that your spirit will never die and that you will experience eternity in heaven with those who have accepted Jesus Christ as Lord of their lives.

NOTES:

August 29
The Ultimate Sacrifice

Isaiah 53:5 (ESV)

There is nothing that we'll ever experience in this life, that is compared to what Christ Jesus endured on the cross of Calvary. You are alive and not dead because Jesus gave up his life for you. You are made whole because Jesus was beaten for every sin that you will ever commit. You receive healing because Jesus endured those whips to his body knowing that through his pain you would be free. There is so much that Jesus endured on the cross that day; be thankful that he did that just for you. Your burdens are now light and your yoke is easy because God sent his only son to die for your sins on the cross.

NOTES:

1 Peter 3:15 (ESV)

It's important to worship Christ as Lord of your life. In doing so you will bring others to Christ through your walk. It's very important to share your testimony. In this, others will begin to see what God is doing in you and through you. If anyone asks about your hope as a believer, be open to explaining it to him or her. Everyone who God has called and chosen to be a part of his kingdom was once a lost soul. So take your time with individuals who want to know how you got to the point you are now, with God. Remember that your walk is only strengthened when you spend time with God. Stay on the potter's wheel so that God can use you, to bring others to his kingdom.

NOTES:

August 31
Align Your Life With Christ

2 Timothy 3:16 (ESV)

The Word of God should be used to bring correction to your life and to help teach you the way that you should go. That is why it's critical to be obedient and to walk in the way of the Lord, allowing your life to align with the will of God. When things in your life are not aligning with the Word of God they are going against God. By reading the Bible it will help you align your life with what God wants for your life. If you're not reading the Bible you won't know what God's plans are for your life. If you don't know the plans God has for you, how can you be walking in purpose? If you aren't walking in purpose, you're not doing what God has called you to do on the earth.

NOTES:

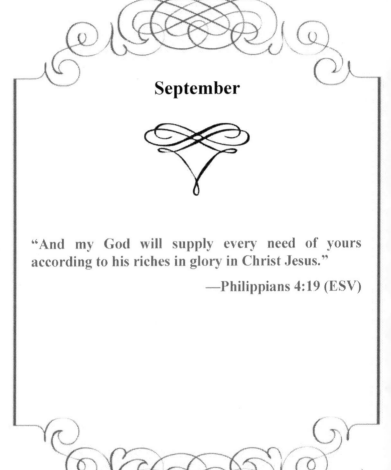

September

"And my God will supply every need of yours according to his riches in glory in Christ Jesus."

—Philippians 4:19 (ESV)

September 1
Your Help Comes From God

Hebrews 12:2 (NIV)

Keep your eyes focused on Jesus, from which your help comes. It is when you take your eyes off Jesus that you begin to see your problems magnify and your situations seem worse than they truly are. When your eyes are focused on Jesus, you will gain a sense of peace, knowing that God is in control of all things. When you keep your eyes on Jesus you will begin to have joy, knowing that God knows the end at the beginning. When you keep your eyes focused on Jesus, you gain hope in the Lord, knowing that through faith God will make things happen on your behalf. When you take your eyes off Jesus, you begin to figure out ways to fix things when you know God doesn't need your help. God is an *on time* God and he will make all things work together for his good.

NOTES:

September 2
Walk In Freedom

1 Peter 5:7 (NIV)

God cares so much about you and he wants you to walk in freedom every day of your life. In order to walk in freedom, you need to cast your cares on Jesus and release your burdens to him. God can't do a full work in you and through you, unless you totally surrender to him; in this you will begin to experience freedom. There are burdens that you are carrying right now that you need to let go of. Identify the burdens that you are carrying and give them to God today. If you want to be free and if you want to fully walk in the purpose that God has for you, let go and let God take total control. Walk in the freedom that God has for you.

NOTES:

September 3
You Are A Masterpiece

Ephesians 2:10 (NIV)

You are God's masterpiece and you were created with a purpose. Everything that God created about you is meant for his good. It's important not to get so caught up in your physical appearance that you forget that God created you as a spiritual being before he gave you an outward shell. Your spirit will spend eternity with Jesus, in heaven, while your physical body will return to dust from which it came. Your physical body was created to die daily while God created your spirit to grow with each passing day. It's essential to know the plan that God has for you, so that what you do in life aligns with his will for your life. You cannot fully walk in the purpose God has for you if you are not doing what God created you to do.

NOTES:

September 4
A Way Of Escape

1 Corinthians 10:13 (ESV)

For every temptation that Satan sends in your direction, God gives you a way to escape. There is no sin on the face of this earth that God is not willing to forgive you of. When you are tempted, know that you will never be tempted beyond your ability. If you are placed in a situation of temptation, there will always be an escape route and you are strong enough to win the battle. Be smart about the decisions that you are making daily; more smart decisions will lead to less temptation. When you hear the still, small voice of the Lord, be obedient to the voice of God so that you will be led in the ways that you should go. God is there to help you with every temptation that you will ever encounter. There is nothing too hard for God.

NOTES:

September 5
Let It Go

Matthew 11:28 (ESV)

It's time to let go of the things that are weighing you down, never to pick them up again, but to lay them at the feet of Jesus so that he can give you sweet rest. You are not able to completely fulfill the will of the Father with a heavy heart. You are not able to completely fulfill the will of the Father with bitterness in your heart. You are not able to completely fulfill the will of the Father with unforgiveness in your heart. It's time to let go of everything that does not allow you to fully fulfill the will of the Father. If it's not good or if it's not meant for good, God does not intend for you to carry it. All things that come from God are good and help you to fulfill his purpose for your life. Let go of everything today that is heavy and weighing you down.

NOTES:

September 6
Don't Dwell On The Past

2 Corinthians 5:17 (ESV)

You are not who you used to be. Once you received Jesus as your Lord and Savior you became a new creature through Christ, putting off the old ways of doing things and choosing to do what God has called you to. Your spiritual eyes are open and you begin to see things in a different light. You begin to have a change of heart, a renewed mind and a renewed spirit through Christ Jesus. Every area of your life that was once darkness has turned into light. People may remember the old you and your old ways, but they will eventually see the change in you and be attracted to the God in you. Don't stop growing in your new nature; you'll never be perfect, but God is certainly working through you.

NOTES:

September 7
Make God Your Priority

Hebrews 13:5 (NIV)

Be free of the love of money. For you cannot love God and love money; one has to take precedence over the other. God should be the top priority in your life; through him everything is possible. There is no reason to try to do things in your own strength when you can go straight to the one that makes all things possible. Everything that money can buy can be supplied through God. Everything that money can't buy is supplied through God. No matter how you perceive things, God is the one who is always in control of all things. Don't get so caught up in this life that you forget about who makes all things possible. Money does not make all things possible. There is no way to buy a relationship with God, nor is there a way to buy your way into heaven. Get your priorities in order, so that you can enjoy the riches and blessings that await you in heaven.

NOTES:

September 8
Weakness Turned Into Strength

2 Corinthians 12:9 (NIV)

Where you are weak, God is strong. This is why God can take your weaknesses and turn them into strengths. Every area that you are weak in, right now, can be turned into strength through Christ Jesus. God's grace is all that you need. It is through time spent with God that you begin to be shaped and molded and are shown the weak areas. From this, allow God to do a new work in you and through you. Individuals will be attracted to you because they can identify with your weaknesses and they will be encouraged at how God turns them into strengths. Your weaknesses are a part of your testimony. It is through the tests that God shows you that where you are weak, he is strong. Share your testimony; it will help save someone's life.

NOTES:

September 9
A Free Gift

Romans 10:9 (ESV)

Salvation is a free gift from God, through Christ Jesus. It is important to confess that Jesus is Lord and to believe that God raised him from the dead, and in doing so, you shall be saved. After you receive the free gift of salvation, the real work begins. You have to build an authentic relationship with Jesus daily so that you do not revert back to your old ways. The devil wants to keep you from fully walking in the life God has for you. God has greatness in store for you, if you just do what it is he has called you to do. Be obedient, stay in your word, pray without ceasing, be a light wherever you go, love God and love people, forgive often, repent daily and align your ways with God's will. God's plan for you is to experience the riches in glory he has in store for you.

NOTES:

September 10
Learn From God Daily

Matthew 11:29 (NLT)

It's important to learn from Jesus in all that he did and all that he was on the earth. Jesus is our prime example, and we should take everything we read about him and apply it to our lives. Jesus showed us that there is nothing too hard for God. Jesus showed us that despite how people treat you, you treat them with love. Jesus showed us that forgiveness is a part of walking in love. Jesus showed us that we are to lead others by his example. Jesus showed us that we are not to give up when times get tough; God will make a way. Jesus showed us that it's important to know your word because Satan knows the Word of God, too. Jesus showed us to not be discouraged, but to ask for help in every situation. Jesus showed us that faith without works is dead. Jesus showed us that trusting him means trusting his timing. Jesus showed us that we are a part of a chosen people. Jesus showed us that obedience is better than sacrifice. Learn from the example of Jesus and apply it to your life today, so that you are walking in the purpose God has for you.

NOTES:

September 11
No Great Thing Withheld

John 15:7 (NLT)

Everything that you ask in the name of the Lord, God wants to give to you. God is not a selfish God, he promised to withhold no good thing from his children. All he asks is that you abide in him and allow his Word to abide in you and whatever you ask in his name will be done. This means that God desires to spend time with you. This means that God commands you to stay in his Word so that his Word will abide in you. This means that if you are obedient to the Word of the Lord he will give you all that you ask of him. There is nothing that God won't do for you; he's able to do exceedingly above anything that you can ask or think.

NOTES:

September 12
Stay Connected To The Source

John 15:4 (NIV)

Through Christ, you are able to reach individuals that in your own strength you would not be able to reach. Staying connected to the source, which is Jesus, allows you to do exceedingly above all that you can ask or think. There are individuals waiting for you to fully blossom into who God has called you to be. From this, you will begin to see lives change because of you. What God places in side of you is not solely for you, it's to reach the masses for his kingdom. When you are willing to do the will of your father you will begin to see greatness birth within you. Don't be afraid of what people will think; they persecuted Jesus too. Don't be afraid of what people will say; they talked about Jesus too. Don't second-guess what God has birthed within you; step out on faith and allow God to carry you the rest of the way.

NOTES:

September 13
Be Used By God

Mark 11:25 (NIV)

Remember that God can use anyone for anything, including you. If you have a teachable spirit and don't have the mind frame that everything has to go your way or no way, God will use you. God will show you things that he has not shown others. God will place in you, things that he has not placed in others. God will use you in ways that he has not used others. Be willing to be childlike when you come to the Father. Have a teachable spirit, have a desire to learn and be willing to do what God has called you to do. Thank God for teaching you what is hidden from the world; it's your time to apply it to your life and to walk in the anointing God has placed over your life.

NOTES:

September 14
Pay Attention

Proverbs 16:20 (ESV)

God intends for you to be successful in this life. In order to be successful you must pay attention to what you are taught. Don't allow what you are being taught from the Word of God to fall on deaf ears. God wants you not only to retain what you are being taught but to also apply it to your life. When you trust in the Lord and his Word you will experience a joy that only comes from God. When you apply God's Word to your life you begin to see how life with Christ is better than your old life. The Word of the Lord is to build you up, to correct you and to help you live the successful life that God has ordained for you.

NOTES:

September 15
Give God The Credit

Proverbs 16:18 (ESV)

Ask God to help you release your prideful nature to him right now. Remember that without God's help you cannot accomplish anything. Everything that has happened in your life, thus far, was because God allowed it to happen. There is nothing that you've achieved outside of the grace of God. Even the things that didn't look so good at first, God turned that around for your good. Don't take credit for what you did not do in your own strength. You are not self-made; you are God made. Everything you are is because God created you. Release, to God, everything about you that is prideful, for pride comes before a fall.

NOTES:

September 16
Submit Your Plan To God

Proverbs 16:9 (ESV)

You can plan out your life according to what you want, but God has the final say in the matter. We get so caught up in what we want out of life, that we forget about what God wants for our lives. God wants you to submit your plans, goals, desires, dreams and ambitions to him. It is only through God that your hearts desires will manifest. If what you want out of life doesn't align with the plans God has for your life, it will never take place. It will benefit you if you allow God in on everything you're doing or about to do so that he can lead and guide you in the way that he wants you to go. Remember, it's not about you; it's about what God is going to do in you and through you. Stay faithful unto death and you will inherit eternal life through Christ Jesus.

NOTES:

September 17
Your Light Attracts Others

Proverbs 16:7 (ESV)

When your life pleases the Lord he will make your enemies at peace with you. There becomes a light about you that attracts individuals to you when you walk in the will of God. There is a change in you and through you that others may not understand but want to be around. When you are loving, kind, and speak of goodness, people are attracted to you. If you don't contribute to the gossip, if you don't respond negatively, if you aren't trying to tear people down, people are attracted to you. If you are living in the world, but not of the world, this pleases God and attracts individuals to you. Don't be discouraged. God will help you walk in greatness all the days of your life.

NOTES:

September 18
Do It God's Way

Proverbs 16:3 (ESV)

God wants to see you succeed, he wants you doing what you love and he wants you to enjoy life. We often get in God's way and think our way is best. Hence the fact that you may not be enjoying life like God intended for you to. For if you commit your work to the Lord you will see your plans be established. This means that whatever your dreams and desires are must to be submitted to God before they can manifest into something great. You can accomplish so much more if you allow God to be the anchor in your life. Your dreams, desires and ambitions matter to God; allow him to take you to new heights in him.

NOTES:

Ephesians 1:4 (NIV)

God chose you. Before the world was made, God chose you and set you apart for his kingdom. Even before you accepted Jesus Christ as Lord and Savior of your life, God chose you. There has been a calling on your life even before you were formed in your mother's womb. You may not fully understand the purpose God has for you, but you have been called to greatness. You may not fully understand why God chose you, but it will be revealed to you. You may not fully understand what you have to do to fully walk in all that God has for you, but if you spend enough time with God he will give you confirmation and revelation. Continue to seek God daily so that you can walk in all that he has for your life.

NOTES:

September 20
Walk In Obedience

Deuteronomy 30:16 (ESV)

It's so important to walk in obedience to the Word of God. There are promises that God will bless us with if we obey his Word. We will be blessed if we walk in love and we will be blessed if we follow the commandments and regulations of God. God promises us that if we do his will we will be blessed. He also warns us that if we don't do the will of our Father there will be consequences to pay. We can live in freedom if we do things God's way instead of doing things our way. God will bless you in all that you do if first you obey what he is calling you to do. You can't get to where you want to go in this life without first doing what God has called you to do.

NOTES:

Proverbs 3:27 (ESV)

There is nothing good that God will withhold from you. In return, God wants you to not withhold good from those whom it is due when it's in your power to do it. This means that if you owe someone something, do not put it off until another day. This means that if God places it on your heart, do it out of the kindness of your heart. This means that you do things not for what people can do for you but because it's the right thing to do. Don't allow what you do for others to be based off what they do for you. If you live by this rule, you're not truly living but merely existing. When you don't withhold any great thing from God's people, God will withhold no great thing from you.

NOTES:

September 22
Be Wise

Proverbs 3:13-14 (NIV)

When you know better, you are supposed to do better. When God imparts wisdom in his children he expects us to gain understanding and walk in his ways. Wisdom is more profitable than anything tangible. If you have wisdom you will know how to deal with things when they come your way. If you have wisdom you will be able to make better decisions in life. Today, ask God to allow you to make wise decisions and to gain understanding. Be wise in your choices from this day forward so that you can live the life God has planned for you. Don't waste the wisdom that God has imparted in you.

NOTES:

September 23
Get Out Of *Self*

Isaiah 61:1-3 (NIV)

What God can do through you is more than you can imagine. God has filled you with his spirit so that you can lead others to him. This means that you have to get out of *self* in order to do the will of God. You have been chosen to bring good news to the poor and to heal broken hearts with the encouraging words that God has placed inside of you. This means that you have to remember that it's not about you, but about whom you'll reach for the Kingdom of God. God has called you to ensure believers that they can walk in freedom because Jesus died on the cross for their sins and they are no longer captives to sin. You are chosen by God to proclaim that God has defeated the enemy and will save anyone who accepts Jesus Christ as their Lord and Savior. You have been called and chosen by God to do a new work in the earth for his kingdom. Continue to strive for greatness.

NOTES:

September 24
Strengthen Your Relationship Daily

Romans 13:14 (ESV)

The stronger your relationship becomes with Jesus, the more you will put on the mind of Christ. You will no longer want to do what your sinful nature tells you to do because you will feel conviction. It's important to put on the mind of Christ and to watch out for the tactics of the enemy. God has a plan for your life and Satan has a plan for your life. You have a choice daily to walk in the light of the Lord or to walk in the darkness that is Satan. God will always give you an escape route when the devil is involved, so make sure that you're paying attention. What God wants for you is more important than indulging in your sinful nature. Sin gives you a temporary high while Jesus gives you a high that only he can bring you down from.

NOTES:

September 25
Love Is A Mandate

Romans 13:9 (GNT)

You have been called by God to love everybody. Loving God and loving people is a mandate by God. When you love, you don't see faces. When you love, you don't hold grudges. When you love, you can forgive easily. When you love, you keep no record of wrong. When you love, you don't judge others. When you love, you see beyond faults. When you love, you mend brokenness. When you love, you choose to trust God. When you love, you walk by faith. This may be an area that you need work in. God wants to help you love everybody, but you have to surrender to God everything that is keeping you from walking in love. Show others the love of Christ today.

NOTES:

September 26
Obey Authority

Romans 13:1 (NLT)

Obey the authority figures that have been placed in your life, by God. For every person, whether a disciple of Christ or not, has been placed in that position by God. There is no authority that exists without God's permission. There may be reasons that we don't want to obey those who have authority over us, but through your obedience you will see all things work together for good. God wants to teach you that through your obedience you will be blessed. Today, repent for not always being obedient to those individuals that God has placed in authority over you and begin to walk in obedience today. From your obedience you will begin to see miracles happen in you, through you and around you.

NOTES:

September 27
Be Positive

Romans 12:21 (ESV)

It's so often that we think on the negative instead of the positive. But today, start thinking differently. Instead of complaining about what's not right, instead of seeing the negative in every situation and instead of worrying, try meditating on positive things. Train your mind to read God's Word daily, train yourself to have an active prayer life and train yourself to have a thankful heart despite what you're going through or have been through. The closer your relationship becomes to God, the more you will see things in a positive light. The more positive you become, the more you will experience peace and joy in abundance. Don't be conformed to this world but be transformed by the renewing of your mind. You were born for this life; walk in purpose.

NOTES:

September 28
Vengeance Is The Lord's

Romans 12:19 (ESV)

You don't have to worry about paying anyone back for the wrong that they have done to you. Why? God declared that vengeance is his and he will repay. Believe that what God has in store for those individuals who have wronged you, is better than anything you could do to them. God is a merciful God and he forgives and will deal with each one of us according to our sins. Don't live to repay individuals for what they've done to you. Be willing to let go and allow God to handle it. Forgive the individuals that have wronged you, hurt you and upset you. God will make all things well.

NOTES:

September 29
Forgiveness Is Freedom

Romans 12:17 (ESV)

Let go of the things that you've been holding on to (acts that individuals have committed against you). Don't think about repaying evil for the evil. God will not only take care of the person who has done evil against you, but he will also take away the hurt and pain that you feel today. If you no longer want to feel hurt and pain today be willing to release those feelings to God. You are to be light in the midst of darkness, and you can't walk in light if you are carrying hatred, bitterness or anger toward someone. Ask God to purge you of everything that is not like him and fill you with his holy spirit and anointing. Live in freedom today—you deserve it.

NOTES:

September 30
Bless And Do Not Curse

Romans 12:14 (ESV)

It's an easy task to love those who you feel are worthy of your love. It is a hard task to bless those who have persecuted you, yet God has called you to do exactly that. You are to bless and not curse or try to get revenge on those individuals who have done wrong to you. Follow the example of Jesus and learn something from his life here on earth. When Jesus was persecuted he didn't lash out, he did not repay evil for evil, he allowed the love of God to be shown through him and he blessed and did not curse. This is exactly what we've been called to do, bless and not curse, no matter what has been done to us. If we put on the mind of Christ we can do this effectively every day of our lives.

NOTES:

October

"God is our refuge and strength, an ever-present help in trouble."

—Psalm 46:1 (NIV)

October 1
Welcome Correction

Proverbs 13:24 (NLT)

Be the child of God that is not opposed to correction. There are things that we do in life that go against what our parents have taught us. A wise child accepts discipline from their parents and from God. Someone who is arrogant refuses to listen to correction. Your life right now can tell you if you've listened to correction or if you've been opposed to being corrected in your life. If you have someone in your life, a parent, pastor, spiritual mentor, teacher, etc. that is helping train you in the way that you should go based on the principles taught in the Word of God, listen carefully. God wants you to be okay with being corrected, no matter how old you are. God has something special in store for you, and it all has to do with your obedience.

NOTES:

October 2
God Is Love

1 Corinthians 13:4-6 (ESV)

What love is according to the Word of God and what love stands for in your life might actually be different things. Ask yourself what your definition of love is and how does that relate to the love that God explains in his Word. God is love. So whatever your definition of love is should be related to who God is. God sees no faces, God keeps no record of wrong, God is patient, God is not arrogant, God is not resentful and God does not rejoice in wrongdoing, but rejoices in the truth. Learn to love everyone by keeping in mind that everything about love is associated with God, because God is love.

NOTES:

October 3
God Makes All Things Possible

Luke 18:27 (ESV)

Always remember that what is impossible with man, is possible with God. What have you been asking God for lately? Restoration, strength, healing, financial breakthrough, mended relationships, courage, new hope, joy, peace, etc. You can have all of these things if first you believe that God can make them possible. You can ask anything in the name of Jesus, always remembering that his name has power. God hears all of your prayers, pleas and petitions. Your breakthrough is on the way. Your miracle is on the way. Your blessings are on the way. Believe that God *can* and he will make all things come together for his good.

NOTES:

October 4
The Narrow Path

Proverbs 2:21-22 (GNT)

Stay on the path that God has for you. For you will live in heaven through eternity, if you continue on the path that God has laid for you. Those who are wicked will not inherit the things of God that you will inherit. It's important to continue building your relationship with Christ daily so that you do not fall into the traps of the enemy that are meant to get you off track. What God has in store for you no eyes have yet seen. Be willing to go the extra mile in doing all that God has called you do to. For your riches in glory do not reside on this earth, they reside in heaven. Live as if you want to see heaven one day.

NOTES:

October 5
Allow God's Word To Shape You

Galatians 6:6 (ESV)

Everything you've learned should be applied to your life in some shape or form. The Word of God allows you to see why things are falling together like they are. The Word of God is meant to correct you in all that you do. The Word of God is meant to encourage you to walk in what God has called you to. The Word of God is meant to show you how to genuinely love and forgive everyone. The Word of God is meant for you to see where obedience gets you and where disobedience will take you. The Word of God is meant to help you step out on faith, even when you don't see the outcome working in your favor. God wants you to share your testimony with others about how you got to the place you are in, by depending on the Word of God. Don't be afraid to share what you've learned and what you intend on learning through the teachings of the Word of God. Let God's Word be your guide in life.

NOTES:

October 6
The Daily Battle

Galatians 5:17 (ESV)

Your spirit and your flesh are in a battle against one another. One wants to do what God wants you to do, while the other wants to do what Satan intends for you to do. You cannot do both; either you walk in the spirit or you walk in the flesh. Every day there is a battle and every day you have a choice to make—whether or not you will walk in what God has called you to or you will walk in what the devil has planned for you. God has a plan for your life and Satan has a plan for your life. What God has in store for you will lead you to abundant life, through eternity. What Satan has in store for you will lead to temporary gain and destruction. Put on the mindset of Christ so that you can walk in what God has ordained for your life.

NOTES:

October 7
Love With No Limit

Galatians 5:14 (ESV)

If we loved everyone else like we love ourselves, the world would possibly be a better place. That is if you truly love yourself, flaws and all. God calls us to love our neighbor as we love ourselves. Everyone that you come in contact with is your neighbor. This means that we are called to love everybody. There is no one exempt from this command; this applies to everyone. Be able to give love, but also receive love. Allow your life to reflect the love of Christ to those around you. Loving others is a beautiful thing, because God is love.

NOTES:

October 8
God Can Turn It Around

Genesis 50:20 (ESV)

What Satan has meant for evil, God can use it for good. Don't worry about the situations that you're dealing with right now, give it to God and watch how he changes things for his good. Just when Satan thinks he prevails, God steps in to intervene and prove that in any situation there is good that can be brought out of it. No matter what you're facing right now, God will show you how he can use it for good. No matter how hard the test is, God intends for you to help someone out of the same storm you just came out of. No matter how much you feel like the victim, right now, God will show you how to prevail in victory. God has a plan for your life and it's good. Whatever Satan has meant for evil God will turn it into good.

NOTES:

October 9
A Life Of Purpose

2 Timothy 1:8-9 (NIV)

God called you to this life. God anointed you for this life. God ordained you for this life. God has a purpose for you in this life that he wants you to fulfill. God has called you to live in holiness. As soon as you're done living life your way, you will begin to see life is better when you live it God's way. No life is an easy life, but living a life led by the Holy Spirit is a life that is sure to bring you peace and joy while you're going through the storms of life. No one is perfect nor will they ever be, but what God has called you to is better than anything the world has to offer you. Live a life of purpose through Christ Jesus, our Lord.

NOTES:

October 10
The Bread Of Life

John 6:35 (ESV)

Everything that you need comes from the Lord. Jesus is the bread of life. Anyone who comes to Jesus will never hunger or thirst again. God will supply all your needs, not only in the spirit but in the physical also. There is not a day that should go by where you aren't in the face of Jesus. If you want to have a stronger relationship with Christ you should ask God to give you the desire to build an authentic relationship with him, daily. In this, you will feel incomplete when you aren't doing what God has called you to do. As you grow in Christ you will notice your appetite for God's Word increase and you will have the desire to get in the presence of God often. Continue to allow God to shape and mold you into the person he wants you to be.

NOTES:

October 11
Redemption

Galatians 3:13 (ESV)

There is power in the blood of Jesus. We are free because Christ died on the cross for our sins. We are no longer under a curse, for the blood of the lamb redeems us. There is nothing that stands in the way of you and the free gift of salvation. Today, thank Jesus for becoming a curse so that you may walk in freedom. Jesus died that you might have life and enjoy it in abundance. Don't take the blood of Jesus for granted—by his stripes you are healed. There is no one in this life that would endure what Jesus endured for each one of us. Because of Jesus, your life is made whole. Walk in freedom today knowing that what Jesus endured has set you totally free.

NOTES:

October 12
A Faith Walk

Galatians 3:10 (NLT)

The righteous shall live by faith. Always remember that faith is essential in this walk. Some people think that their good deeds are all that matters, but God said it is not by your works, but by faith that he will give you what he has promised you. Think of it this way, accepting Jesus Christ was not done by works but by believing (having faith). This is what we have to practice daily. Not to say that you shouldn't do good deeds, or you shouldn't work hard. It's to say that your faith outweighs your deeds because your deeds solely will not get you the promises God has for you. It is my prayer that every individual reading this will have faith as a mustard seed. Bless them with miracles, favor, peace and prosperity, in Jesus' name, Amen.

NOTES:

October 13
Receive Revelation

Galatians 1:12 (NLT)

If you spend enough time with Jesus you will receive revelation that no human can give you. We are so caught up in asking our friends and family things that we should direct straight to God. It is understood that you want answers quickly, but what better way than to go straight to the source that holds the answers to everything. In spending time with God you will realize that he gives confirmation, revelation and affirmation. Sit there long enough not just to talk, but also to listen. There is nothing that God will hide from you, there is nothing that God will withhold from you and there is nothing that God will tell you, to send you in the wrong direction. Spend more time with Jesus daily and you are guaranteed to see a transformation in your life.

NOTES:

October 14
Cry Out To God

Psalm 30:2 (ESV)

There are times when the only thing we can do is cry out to the Lord for help. When you cry out to God, he hears you and he will heal you. Have faith that your pleas, prayers and petitions are not in vain. Sometimes God takes a little while to answer our prayers while other times our prayers are answered immediately. Don't worry about when God will answer you; it will be in his timing. We serve an *on time* God. Don't feel like God has counted you out because you aren't receiving the answer to every prayer you've ever prayed. God has never stopped working on your behalf. When you cry out to God you have to sit long enough to hear the voice of God respond back to you. Pray, listen and be obedient to the Word of the Lord.

NOTES:

October 15
The Armor Of God

2 Corinthians 2:11 (ESV)

God will make you aware of the schemes of the enemy if you ask him to. Each day there is a plan set up for your life, from the enemy. This plan is to kill, steal and destroy you by any means necessary. Wake up each day with the armor of God on and proclaim that the devil will not win over your life. What God has planned for your life does not include anything that the devil has to offer. Ask God to teach you the tactics and schemes of the enemy, so that you do not walk into the traps that he sets for your life daily. Each trap that is set for your life by the enemy, God has already given you an exit strategy. You have to have a keen ear to hear with clarity, so that every trap that is laid for you will be made known to you. Walk in the plan God has for you by outsmarting the enemy and his tactics daily.

NOTES:

October 16
Renew Your Mind Daily

Isaiah 55:9 (ESV)

It is imperative that you put on the mindset of Christ Jesus. When you put on the mindset of Christ you will notice that your thoughts are not his thoughts and your ways are not his ways. This is important to realize because when you put on the mindset of Christ you tend to make better decisions, you tend to use better judgment, you tend to use wisdom, you tend to seek the voice of God before making decisions in your life. Some of the things that are going wrong in your life are because you have not taken time out to listen to what God is saying to you. You have not stopped to ask God any questions. You are so busy thinking the way you want to think and doing the things you want to do. Today, God wants you to remember that his ways are better than your ways and his thoughts are better than your thoughts. Change your mindset and it will change your life.

NOTES:

October 17
A Cleanse From Within

Isaiah 55:8 (ESV)

There is something new that God wants to do in you. It has to start from within so that it can shine on the outside. Ask God to help you think pure thoughts, to help you eliminate the negative that you've spoken over your life, to help you eliminate doubt, to help you eliminate fear and to help you eliminate the feeling of inferiority. God can and will change your way of thinking. Everything that you have said or thought over your life that is negative, God wants to turn into a positive. God thinks so highly of you and wants you to start thinking highly of yourself. God wants you to start walking in the anointing that he has ordained over your life. Your way of doing things is not getting you to the places God has called you to. Lean not on your own understanding, but seek the face of God daily so that you know what the next steps are, to take in this life. God wants to take you to new heights in him. Get out of your own way and do it God's way.

NOTES:

October 18
Be Light Wherever You Go

Colossians 1:13-14 (NIV)

You have been delivered from the darkness of the world and now walk in light as a child of God. It is because you have accepted Jesus Christ as your Lord, that you receive the free gift of salvation and are forgiven for your sins. You are to walk in light and to be an example of Christ on the earth for the rest of your days while here on earth. It's important to remember that wherever you go, you bring the presence of God with you. You were brought out of darkness to help someone else find his or her way to the light. Don't compare your walk or even your testimony with others. God has led you on the path that you are on, to reach the individuals you are supposed to reach for his kingdom. You were born for this life; walk in the greatness that God has in store for you.

NOTES:

October 19
A Work In Progress

Colossians 1:10-12 (ESV)

Be steadfast and immovable, always relying on the spirit of God to lead and guide you. You may not know what is coming ahead, but we serve a God that is the creator of what lies ahead. Remember that your road to heaven was never promised to be without bumps and potholes. Allow everything that you go through to grow you spiritually and mentally. If everything came easy, you wouldn't be as strong as you are today. Learn to pray without ceasing and yearn to feel God's presence daily. You are a work in progress, be proud of that. Continue to allow God to shape and mold you daily so that you are everything he wants you to be as you follow him in all that you do. God has given you the strength and courage to endure. Walk in purpose.

NOTES:

October 20
Never Stop Seeking God

Proverbs 2:4-6 (GNT)

There should never be a time in this life where you stop seeking God. When you seek God with your whole heart you will gain wisdom, knowledge and understanding in all things that you are made aware of by God. When seeking God with your whole heart, you will succeed at learning about God and his ways of doing things. God never tries to hide himself from you. In fact, he's always near, and his presence can always be felt if you just take some time out and bask in it. God wants you to seek him so that you can feel his heartbeat and be on one accord with him. Never stop seeking the greatness that is God; in him you will find your being.

NOTES:

October 21
Your Ordained Life

Psalm 27:4 (GNT)

In order to enjoy the riches and glory that God has for you in heaven, you must do the things that he has called you to do here on earth. We should not think that we could be disobedient all the days of our lives on earth and enjoy the blessings that God promises us when we leave this earth. It doesn't work that way. Yes, you have given your life to Christ, but are you walking in the life that Christ ordained for you? There is still work to be done on your part on the earth. It's called purpose! Once God has revealed your purpose to you, walk in it. You only have a certain amount of seconds, minutes, hours, days and years to complete your task here on earth. Your life is worth living so make it count.

NOTES:

October 22
Spiritual Growth

James 1:22 (ESV)

The Word of God is meant for you to put it into practice. Allow your talk about Jesus to match your walk with Jesus. Many individuals are watching you to see if what you say about who Jesus is to you, matches how you live believing in that same Jesus. More importantly, don't allow the Word of God to fall on deaf ears. Don't just hear the Word, but apply the Word of God to your life. When you can apply the Word of God to your life, that's called growth. When you're growing you're moving forward in life, even if it's just a few steps at a time. The Bible is your guide to life. Any question or scenario that you can possibly think of is in the Word of God. Starting today, practice applying the Word of God to your life. You will be a witness of God working miraculously in you, through you and around you.

NOTES:

October 23
Quick To Listen, Slow To Speak

James 1:19-20 (ESV)

God has given you two ears and one mouth for a reason. Before you speak, God wants you to be quick to listen. When you avail yourself to hearing God you will be able to walk in the plan that God has for you. When you avail yourself to hearing God you will be able to recognize the voice of God without questioning it. When you avail yourself to hearing God you will make wiser decisions on a daily basis. Be willing to listen before speaking so that you can hear with clarity, everything that God is speaking to you. Go before God daily, in prayer, with a humble heart and open ears to receive the instructions that he has for you. Take nothing that God says for granted. Greatness, freedom, wisdom, blessings, deliverance, favor and goodness will come when you adhere to the voice of God.

NOTES:

October 24
Each Day Is A Surprise

James 1:17 (ESV)

There are gifts bestowed upon you daily. Each day is a surprise and it entails a new gift. Learn not to take for granted what you have today because tomorrow is not promised to you. Live in the *right now*, be thankful for the gifts of today and be grateful that God chose you to share in these gifts. Everything that is good comes from God and is a gift from God. Thank God for the many gifts that he bestows on you daily. The gift of life, the gift of love, the gift of family, the gift of friends, the gift of marriage, the gift of freedom, the gift of prosperity, the gift of laughter, the gift of joy, the gift of peace, the gift of sanity, the gift of good health, etc. Enjoy the gifts that God bestows on you daily, cherish them and embrace them.

NOTES:

October 25
Christ Centered Vs. World Centered

Luke 18:24-25 (NIV)

The focus of this world is on two things money and power. When your main focus in life is on money and power you spend less time with God and more time trying to get money and gain power. It's essential to constantly build your relationship with Christ so that you are Christ centered, instead of world centered. There is nothing wrong with wanting to be well off, but there is something wrong with stepping on God's toes to get there. Through Christ Jesus, anything is possible. Knowing that God holds everything in the palm of his hands should give you a push to build your relationship with him, so that he can give you all that your heart desires. God will make your heart pure and bestow on you all the promises he has for you. Stop trying to do things in your own strength and allow God to give you what he wants for you when he wants you to have it. Rely on God and do not lose hope on the journey to your destiny.

NOTES:

October 26
You Have Been Accepted

Romans 10:13 (NIV)

You are accepted. Yes, you! The choice is ultimately up to you, whether or not you will accept Jesus Christ as Lord of your life. Jesus has already accepted you. God sent Jesus for the sinner—which means you. So don't think you need to have it all together, don't think you need to be perfect and don't think that the sins you have committed can't be forgiven. Our God is a merciful God and he wants you to live in eternity with him. The choice is yours. There is never a right or wrong time; God's arms are always open to you. The free gift of salvation will always be offered to you through Christ Jesus. Accept Jesus Christ in your heart today and be saved. Leave your old life in the past and walk in the greatness that God has in store for you. Continue to strive for greatness.

NOTES:

October 27
Spend Quality Time

Philippians 4:7 (ESV)

God wants to bestow on you peace that surpasses all understanding. When you get into the face of God, you will realize that true peace only comes from God. If you are not experiencing peace on a consistent basis, you have not been spending enough time with God. If you feel burdened, overwhelmed or imprisoned right now, you have not been spending enough time with God. God is always in your presence; all you need to do is set time aside time so that you hear the Holy Spirit speaking life into you at every second of every moment. True peace does not come from having stuff, things and people in your life. True peace comes from having an authentic relationship with the true and living God, the one who created you and who created peace. When you experience peace that surpasses all understanding, you have experienced God on a supernatural level.

NOTES:

October 28
No More Fear

2 Timothy 1:7 (ESV)

God no longer wants you to live your life in fear—fear from the unknown, fear of failure and fear of not being good enough. God has given you the spirit of power, of love and a sound mind. You are important to God, what you do in life is important to God, how you live your life is important to God and who you choose to become, in this life, is important to God. You can't be afraid to live up to your full potential, you can't be afraid to step out on faith, you can't be afraid to trust God, you can't be afraid to love, you can't be afraid to forgive and you can't be afraid to step away from the crowd and do what God has called you to do. God has called you, he has chosen you and he has anointed you for this life. The spirit of fear comes from the pit of hell to hinder your walk, to make you revert back to who you used to be and to stop your growing process. Recognize when the spirit of fear creeps up on you and cast it back to the pit of hell from which it came. You shall no longer live in fear from this day forward, in Jesus' name.

NOTES:

October 29
The Ultimate Price

2 Corinthians 5:21 (NLT)

There was a price that Christ paid for our sins, knowing that his blood would put us in right standing with God. There is no one in this world that would die for you the way Christ did. He came to this earth that you may be saved, he came to this earth that you may know what true love is, he came to this earth that you may know what forgiveness is and he came to this earth to show you how to be selfless. God loves you so much that he sacrificed his only son, that you may experience eternal life through Christ Jesus. No matter what you've done in your life and no matter what you've been through, God is still God and his love for you has been proven daily since the day you were in your mother's womb. The price paid by Jesus Christ for your life should make you live life in abundance, knowing that you will experience a lifetime in eternity.

NOTES:

October 30
Quality Time In God's Presence

Romans 15:13 (NLT)

It cannot be stressed enough that it is important to spend time with God. This is time set aside in a place of solitude, where only God resides. This is a place where you surrender all to God, where you take off the mask, where you pour your heart out to God with no limit on time and no limit on the things that you express to him. In this place you will find new hope, in this place you will find peace and in this place you will find joy. A new hope will be found in this place of solitude, as well as direction and confirmation. All it takes is a set time and a determined heart on your part. The devil will try to distract you from getting to this place, but you will see the difference in your walk and in your talk when you meet God in that place of solitude. What you do in secret, God shall reward you openly.

NOTES:

October 31
You Shall Live And Not Die

John 11:25 (ESV)

Through Christ Jesus you shall live and not die. We all will experience a natural death where our bodies return to dust from which it came, but we shall live and not die. As children of God our salvation allows our spirit to continue to live through eternity and experience the riches and blessings that God has in store for us. So even if you die a natural death, as a child of God you will embark on a new journey through Christ Jesus and experience a life that is better than this life on earth. So don't focus too much on the life that you live now because life after death is the life that you are truly living for. Don't get so caught up with this world and what it has to offer. For what God has in store for you is greater than what this world could ever offer you. Jesus promised that if you believe in him, though you die, you shall live. Walk in freedom today, knowing that as a child of God you shall live and not die.

NOTES:

November

"So now I am giving you a new commandment. Love each other. Just as I have loved you, you should love each other."

—John 13:34 (NLT)

November 1
Increased Faith

Hebrews 11:6 (ESV)

There is no way to please God in this walk, if you do not have faith. For whoever comes to God must have faith that he exists and that he rewards those who seek him. As you continue building your relationship with Christ you will begin to notice the level of your faith increase. This is because you will begin to see God move miraculously in you, through you and around you. As you surrender your life to Christ and seek after him, you will begin to notice your heart change, your mind change and your spirit being transformed. Continue to strive for greatness, knowing that what God has in store for you is better than anything you can get yourself. Continue to walk by faith, allowing God to take total control over your life. While God is in control you'll notice things begin to align with God's will. What God has in store for you is amazing; continue to seek after him like never before.

NOTES:

November 2
Your Choices In Life Matter

Isaiah 53:6 (NIV)

God has a plan for your life. There is a choice that needs to be made by you daily—whether to follow God's path or to follow your own path. Where you end up in life is ultimately the result of what path you chose to take in life—God's path or your own. As the result of Jesus dying on the cross for your sins, you will be welcomed back in right standing with God, no matter how long you've taken your own path. Make the conscious decision today to get back in right standing with God. Notice how far you get when you're leading yourself, notice how hard the road becomes when you're leading yourself, and notice how many times you've gone in a circle and still have not arrived at your destination when you're leading yourself. When you follow the path God has laid out for you, it will lead you to your destiny.

NOTES:

November 3
Created In God's Image

Genesis 1:27 (NIV)

You were created in the image of God. God took precious time to form you, shape you and mold you into who he wanted you to be. It's an insult to God when you don't love yourself the way that he created you. Don't let the world dictate to you what looks good, God already created you and everything that he created is good. So take a look in the mirror and accept everything about yourself, flaws and all. If God wanted anything about you to be different, he would have created you with what you feel you're lacking. Don't try and be God over your life. It's important to love you for you, knowing that God created you with a purpose and in his image. Love thyself like God loves you.

NOTES:

November 4
Greatness Awaits You

Colossians 3:12 (GNT)

You have been called and chosen by God. This means that you are a part of a royal priesthood. What God has called you to, is greater than anything that you can imagine. God is calling you to be an example of him on the earth. When you seek after what God has for you, you will begin to walk in purpose. You have been called to walk in holiness, to show compassion to those that you encounter on a daily basis, to be kind no matter the situation, to humble yourself before God and others so that God can exalt you and to be patient waiting on the Lord to move through you at every second of every day. Don't doubt that God is working in you and through you. Walk in love, be authentic, share Jesus without fear, and surrender all to God so that he can move through you. Your best days are ahead of you.

NOTES:

November 5
Time To Let It Go

Hebrews 12:1 (ESV)

There is a race that you're running, and in order to keep the pace God has set for you, you need to let go of everything that is weighing you down. Let go of the sins that are so easily tripping you up, the burdens that are a hurdle in front of you, the fear that you're not capable and the doubt that someone is more qualified. What God has for you is for you, no one can take that away from you. God has placed individuals in your life to push you to the finish line; don't give up now. The race gets tough at different points, but God has equipped you to finish the race. Once the weights have been lifted, you will notice that you can endure more than you've ever imagined. Keep running, keep pushing and keep your eyes focused on Jesus. Strive for greatness.

NOTES:

November 6
Prayer Can Change Anything

James 5:16 (NIV)

Prayer changes things. It's important not only to pray for yourself, but to allow others to pray for you also. The prayer of a righteous person has great power. Expect God to move on your behalf, once you spend time with him in prayer. There is nothing that God can't do for you. The more time you spend with God, in prayer, the more you become aware of his miraculous powers. Make it a point to spend time with God daily. Don't do it as a religious activity, do it because you want an authentic relationship with Christ. Prayer is your lifeline to God.

NOTES:

November 7
Failure Is Not An Option

Philippians 4:19 (NIV)

There is no reason for you to doubt God. He knows what you need, what you want and what you desire. God has never failed you and he won't start now. Believe that God can do the impossible; there are miracles that happen all around you daily. When you doubt God and doubt if he will come through for you, it's a slap in the face to him. If ever you felt let down by God, you haven't realized the bigger picture. What God has for you, is for you, and he will not allow it to pass you by. Take a leap of faith, don't take your eyes off God and be thankful that God knows the end, at the beginning.

NOTES:

November 8
Be A Great Example

John 1:1 (NLT)

God sent his only son, Jesus Christ, to the earth to become flesh as an example for us here on earth. It's important to remember that God is the Word, and if God is the Word and he lives in your heart, you represent the Word of God. This means that you should have a desire to get the Word of God in your heart, mind and spirit daily because someone is reading you like the Bible. Jesus Christ was our example here on earth. Now it's time for you to be an example for others on the earth so that you can lead them to Christ through his Word. The more you saturate yourself in the Word of God, the more you will become Christ-like.

NOTES:

November 9
We're Better Together

Psalm 133:1 (ESV)

We, as the body of Christ, are stronger together than we are apart. God has called us to dwell in unity. Your function in the body is as beneficial as the next person. It's important to work together and to realize that your part does matter. You are called, you are chosen and you have a purpose. Work together with others that are like-minded to bring those who are lost, to Christ. Be willing to work together with others for the common good of winning souls to the Kingdom of God. Everyone has a major part to play; if you aren't contributing the body of Christ is not functioning properly.

NOTES:

November 10
God Has The Final Say

Micah 6:8 (GNT)

The results you get out of life are based on your relationship with the one true and living God. God has set up requirements, commands and rules for you to follow. If you don't know the Word of God for yourself, you probably don't know what standard God has set for you. If you don't know the standard God has set for you, you aren't living up to your full potential. If you aren't living up to your full potential, you aren't walking in your God-given purpose. If you aren't walking in your purpose, you aren't living the life God has planned for you. You see, life is not what you make it. Life is only given and taken away by God. You can try to lead yourself, but in the end God has the final say.

NOTES:

November 11
Your Test Turned Into A Testimony

John 1:12 (ESV)

Your life with Christ depends on your acceptance and your belief in Jesus Christ. You don't have to have it all together to be a child of God. God will take all that you've been through, all that you've done and all that you've seen in life and turn it into good. Don't doubt that God can take your test and turn it into an effective testimony. God is waiting to use you to win souls to his kingdom. God is waiting for you to share your testimony without being fearful of who will judge you. God is waiting for you to be self-*less* so that he can use you to do his work on the earth wholeheartedly. When you said yes to be a child of God, you said yes to be a willing vessel for the sake of God's kingdom. Allow God to use you in ways he has never used you before.

NOTES:

November 12
Remain Faithful During The Test

James 1:12 (ESV)

Remain steadfast and immovable when God tests you. If you can succeed at passing the tests that God sets in front of you, not only will you have a great testimony but you will also receive the life that God has promised you. Don't get discouraged that things may not be going exactly how you planned them. God's plan is neither your plan, nor are his thoughts your thoughts. If you can remain faithful during the tests, you show God that you trust him. If you've never gone through anything in life, you would not be as strong as you are now. Things seem hard until God shows you the way to overcome the obstacle. Don't allow Satan to win. The battle is not yours; it's the Lord's.

NOTES:

November 13
Fellowship Is Important

Hebrews 10:25 (NLT)

It's important to fellowship regularly with like-minded individuals who are Christ-like. This is important so that you can stay encouraged and also encourage someone else. There are individuals who need to know that you made it out of the storm, there are individuals who need to know how you made it out of the storm and there are individuals who need to know what you did during the storm. Your testimony does matter! Meeting together with others on a regular basis to discuss how the Holy Spirit works in your life, can help transform and change a life. It's by your testimony that you draw others to Christ. Walk in love all the days of your life.

NOTES:

November 14
Never Second Guess God

2 Peter 1:4 (ESV)

God will fulfill every promise that he has made to you. Leave no room for second guessing the things that God has placed in front of you to be accomplished. What God has for you, is for you, and it will not pass you by. Stay dedicated to the Word of God so that you know what God has in store for you. God can provide everything that you want out of life. Don't be so caught up in what the world offers, tap into what God has to offer you, which will last through eternity. When what you want out of life aligns with God's will for your life, it will take place. Learn to plug into the source (Jesus Christ) so that everything in your life is done according to God's will for your life.

NOTES:

November 15
Realize Your Full Potential

Philippians 1:6 (ESV)

God wants you to realize your full potential. What God has placed inside of you, shall be accomplished before you leave this earth. It's up to you to realize how special you are to God and how he wants to use you for his glory on the earth. Everything that God has placed in your heart, he will bring to completion if you trust him and align it with his will for your life. There is something special about you, and he has placed something unique in your heart to be accomplished. Although there is nothing new done under the sun, the Lord wants to use you in fresh and new ways to complete the task that he has set for you. Don't get discouraged on this journey. God is up to something. Don't doubt what God can do in you and through you.

NOTES:

November 16
Thank God For Jesus

Acts 4:12 (ESV)

The one person who could save us died on the cross for our sins and shed his blood that we may have life and have it abundantly. There is no other person who has walked this earth that can give you the free gift of salvation, but Jesus Christ. Thank God for sending his son, Jesus, to die for your sins. Every day should be a day of thanksgiving, knowing that Jesus was beaten, persecuted, spit on and nailed to the cross for you. There is no one but Jesus who would endure that pain for you. Make it a point each day to thank God for Jesus and thank Jesus for his selflessness on the cross. His shed blood will cover you all the days of your life.

NOTES:

November 17
Perfect Peace

Isaiah 26:3 (ESV)

It's important to build an authentic relationship with Jesus Christ. In building this relationship you will begin to thirst after his Word like never before. Not only to know the scriptures but to actually apply the scriptures to your personal life. It's not to say that you will never go through things, but you will now know how to deal with the things that you face daily, based on what you've read. God will keep you in perfect peace because you trust him in everything that you do. When your mind is focused on Jesus, it's like a high that you never come down from. Try spending more time with God and see how much more peaceful your life truly becomes.

NOTES:

November 18
Live In Holiness

1 Peter 2:24 (NIV)

Transform your mind to think like Christ. Jesus bore our sins that we might die to sin and live to righteousness. The world does not want you to be holy by its standards, but God has called you to holiness. You have been set apart, you are a part of a royal priesthood, you are the head and not the tail, you are above and not beneath. What Jesus did for each one of us is nothing short of amazing. Because he died, you get to live. So today, LIVE! Don't just merely exist in this world. Do what you know God has called you to do. Be whom you know God has called you to be. Go where you know God has called you to go. Start truly living from this day forward.

NOTES:

November 19
You Have The Authority

Matthew 28:18 (NIV)

There is power in using the authority that God has given you to win souls for his kingdom. The same way that people listened to Jesus Christ, is the same way that individuals are listening to you right now. Make sure that what you are putting out in the atmosphere is coming from God. You don't want to lead anyone astray based on what you tell them about God, Jesus Christ, the Holy Spirit or the Word of God (the Bible). It's very critical in these last days to stay in your word and live the Word of God to the best of your ability. The anointing on your life has been placed on you, from God, to do the will of God. God has set you apart; walk in your God-given purpose.

NOTES:

November 20
Be A Reflection Of Love

Matthew 22:37 (ESV)

The Lord God commands you to love him with all your heart, all your soul and all your mind. When you love God wholeheartedly, he teaches you to love yourself as well as loving others as he loves them. God is the definition of love. If God truly lives in your heart then your life should exhibit love. There should be no excuse or reason you should not love someone. God sent his son, Jesus Christ, to the earth to show us the true definition of what love is. Love sees no faces, love keeps no record of wrong, love is patient, love is kind, and love never fails. If you have a relationship with God, you know what true love is. Begin to walk in love all the days of your life, from this day forward.

NOTES:

November 21
Light Cast Out Darkness

Matthew 5:16 (NLT)

Allow your light to shine. Light will cast out darkness when it steps on the scene. You should always think of yourself as light, if you're a child of God. When you step on the scene you change the atmosphere. People are watching you, they are mimicking what you do and even the things that you say, and someone out there wants to be just like you. So make sure that you're being the best example of Christ that you possibly can. This does not mean that you will be sinless, but it does mean that you try sinning less. Being aware of the light that is shown through you means, that you're aware of God working in you and through you. God has chosen you to exalt him on the earth and because of this his name will be glorified.

NOTES:

November 22
There Is A Way To Escape

Hebrews 4:15 (ESV)

One of the many great things about Jesus Christ is that he sympathizes with our weaknesses. It's not as if Jesus was not ever tempted by Satan as we are each day of our lives. Jesus showed us that despite being tempted by the devil, there is always a way of escape. Knowing that you will be tempted, most times with the very things that you love, should help you realize that if Jesus was tempted and didn't sin, you can be tempted and not sin. You will have moments of weakness and it will sometimes be hard to walk away from things that look good, feel good and smell good. But God! Learn to be in control of yourself at all times, with the help of the Lord. Don't allow Satan to continue to steal, kill and destroy you and keep you in the sins that you are trying so hard to fight against. You are stronger than you think.

NOTES:

November 23
Follow The Example Of Jesus Christ

John 13:35 (ESV)

The command that God gives us is to "Love" so that people know that you are a disciple of Christ Jesus. Out of faith, hope, and love, love is the greatest of them. Loving everyone shows that despite what they did to you, you can forgive them.

Are you capable of loving everyone?

Indeed you are, or Jesus would have not made it a command. You see, this command is set in place so that you will follow the example of Jesus Christ. He showed you what it takes to love everyone despite who they are, what they've done, who they're associated with, etc. God has called us to love, despite people being unlovable, despite people being unchangeable, despite people not showing love back to you. God has called you to love everyone. Loving everyone shows that God lives in you and that you are a part of him. Stop using the excuse that God knows your heart and ask God to show you how to love everyone. Love does not see faces. Love sees spirit and the need of the person.

NOTES:

November 24
Building An Authentic Relationship

Psalm 34:8 (ESV)

Once you've experienced the goodness and fullness of the true and living God, it's something that you don't want to go a day without. Building an authentic relationship with God allows you to experience him in fresh and new ways daily. Not by force, not by obligation, not as part of a religious experience, but you begin to desire a true authentic relationship with your creator. During the lifetime of getting to know Jesus for yourself you'll recognize your purpose, you'll recognize the anointing over your life, you'll recognize the calling over your life, you'll see things from a different perspective, you'll gain clarity and understanding, you'll learn to live the Word of God, you'll learn to love God wholeheartedly and to love others, you'll learn to be obedient and you'll learn to hear the voice of God and align your ways with his will. God wants you to experience his goodness all the days of your life.

NOTES:

November 25
No Limit To Loving Others

1 Corinthians 13:13 (NLT)

There is no limit on the love that God shows to you daily, so there should be no limit when you show love to others. God wants you to love more than you have faith in anything. God wants you to love more than you have hope in anything. Love is a big deal to God. It's such a big deal that loving God and loving people are commandments given to us, by God. It's such a big deal that God sent his son, Jesus Christ, to give us an example of what loving God and loving people truly look like. Don't be so caught up in your life and your issues that you forget about what God has called you to do on earth. It may not be an easy task, but God has set it as a command because he knows that you can achieve it.

NOTES:

November 26
God Is Working On Your Behalf

Jeremiah 32:27 (ESV)

Knowing who God is and what he's capable of will allow you to trust him like never before. Knowing that he is creator of all things and that he knows all things, and that there is nothing too hard for God will allow you to trust him like never before. Many things may seem impossible to man but there is nothing that is impossible with God. Anything that you can ever imagine and ever ask for is possible with God. God wants you to trust him like never before, knowing that he has everything under control. God is working behind the scenes on your behalf and he knows exactly what needs to take place. Take a step back and remember that everything you dream of, everything you desire, everything you want out of life is not too hard for God. Submit your plans to God and watch them be established, if they align with his will for your life.

NOTES:

November 27
Trust Your Creator

Isaiah 50:10 (NIV)

There was once a time in your life where you were in darkness, before you came to accept Jesus Christ as Lord of your life. As you walk in light, the rest of the days of your life, learn to trust your creator. Learn to hear the voice of God with clarity and gain understanding from his Word as you read. Allow God to change your mind, change your heart and change your spirit daily, as you grow closer to him with each passing day. Your life is not your own and each day you awake is not about you. You live because God has an assignment for you here on earth. You may not understand it now, but your purpose here on earth is bigger than you. Consult God on everything you do so that you're being used for his glory and not your own.

NOTES:

Philippians 1:21 (ESV)

If you're truly living and not just existing, you're living for Christ. When you chose to be a child of God, you chose to be a reflection of God on the earth. Not by your standards, not by the world's standards, but by God's standards. This means that you learn to die to self, because it's not about you. This means that you listen to the voice of God over your own conscious and do what he has called you to do. This means that sometimes you may feel lonely, because you aren't conforming to the world. This means that you trust God with your whole heart no matter what the problem looks like in front of you. You have been called. You have been chosen. You have been set apart. You have been anointed. What God wants to do in you and through you is more than you can imagine. Don't lose hope. Strive for greatness.

NOTES:

Matthew 7:7 (ESV)

God promises to never withhold anything from his children. When you ask God for anything, make sure that your heart is pure and that you're not trying to use it for your own selfish desires. When you ask, make sure that you're ready to receive from God what he wants to give you, in his perfect timing. Don't go seeking things that you really aren't ready for. For when you seek, God will allow you to find everything that you were seeking him for and more. Every opportunity that comes your way is not always an opportunity sent by God. Allow God to open the doors that he wants you to walk through. When you knock and it's God, the door will be opened for you. God is waiting to bless you in miraculous ways.

NOTES:

November 30
It's A Growing Process

Romans 8:18 (ESV)

If you had a sneak-peek of what God has in store for you in heaven, you probably would not complain about what's going on with you in this present day. Nothing can compare to what God has in store for his children. It's important that you realize that this world is not the end. What you're going through right now is not the end. What you will endure in the future is not the end. One thing is for sure God is still God today, tomorrow and forevermore. The Word of God warns that you will suffer for the sake of Jesus Christ. Better to suffer years in this world, than to suffer through eternity all the days of your spiritual life. You're not the only one being tested daily, going through storms or being tempted. Trust God through the process, increase your faith each day and remember that what awaits you in heaven, is better than any monetary thing that is on the face of this earth.

NOTES:

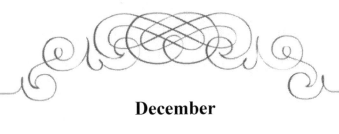

December

"Trust in the Lord with all your heart, and do not lean on your own understanding. In all your ways acknowledge him, and he will make straight your paths."

—Proverbs 3:5-6 (ESV)

December 1
Steadfast And Immovable

1 Corinthians 15:57-58 (ESV)

You have the victory. God gave you the victory the moment he sent Jesus Christ to die on the cross for your sins. Stop giving up so easily, when things aren't going your way. Stand firm in your faith, being steadfast and immovable. There will be a lot of things that come your way, things that you're not sure how to deal with. But God! It all comes down to trusting God and believing that the outcome is already in your favor because you are a child of God. Continue to do the work of God, all the days of your life, knowing that if it's for God it's not useless and your labor is not in vain. Live a life that is pleasing to God and he shall give you the victory.

NOTES:

December 2
A Test Of Faith

Psalm 23:4 (ESV)

What you face in life is not meant to break you, but to help you trust God even more. There has never been a time in your life where God has forsaken you, turned his back on you or left you. Every situation you face, God is right there. Every battle you fight, God is guiding you. Every test you were faced with, God helped you pass. In your darkest hour, God is the light that leads you to safety. You are never alone. Draw close to God and God will draw close to you. Your strength comes from God. Your help comes from God. Your endurance comes from God. Your power comes from God. Your light comes from God. God is always there to lead, guide and protect you. Every day of your life learn to tap into the source from which your help comes from.

NOTES:

December 3
Knowledge Is Power

Proverbs 1:7 (NLT)

Respect the Lord and take heed to his teachings. God did not send his son Jesus as an example for us so that we could do the opposite of what he has taught us. God did not create the Bible for us so that we would go against everything that it stands for. Remember that knowledge is power. The more knowledge that you retain from the Word of God, the more equipped you will be to stand against the enemy. Everything that you will ever face in life is found in the Bible, there is nothing new under the sun. Everything that will happen to you in this lifetime has already taken place with someone in the Bible. When you hide the Word of God in your heart, it will not depart from you.

NOTES:

December 4
Change Your Mind, Change Your Life

Psalm 19:14 (NLT)

Allow God to take total control of who you are. This means that what you think is like God, what you speak comes from God and what you do are the things that God has planned for you to do. You want a better life, but are you willing to do what it takes to get it? First, you have to ask God to change your heart. Everything that is not like God, needs to be removed before you can fully walk in your destiny. Second, you have to change your mind. Ask God to purge every negative thought and transform it into a positive thought that comes from him. Change your mind and you will change your life. God has instilled greatness within you and Jesus has already validated you.

NOTES:

December 5
Gain Clarity And Understanding

2 Timothy 2:7 (NLT)

God is not a God of confusion. Whenever you are feeling confused or uncertain of a situation, ask God for understanding. The Lord will give you understanding about everything. It's important to allow the Holy Spirit to be the first point of reference when you don't understand something. Make it a point to go to God before you ask a parent, a spouse, a family member or a friend. We think those closest to us hold the answers to almost everything, but this is not the case. Only the creator of all things holds the answer to every question and concern that you have. God rejoices when you come to him with your prayers, pleas, petitions, questions and concerns. You are guaranteed to gain clarity and understanding when you spend time with God.

NOTES:

December 6
There Is Power In Prayer

Mark 14:38 (NIV)

There is a daily battle that you have to fight. For where your spirit is willing to fight the battle, your flesh is often weak. God always offers you an escape route when you are tempted with temptation, and prayer plays a big part. Don't underestimate the power of prayer. God says, keep watch and pray. He has warned you that the devil will tempt you. Jesus also gave us an example of how we can escape the temptation without giving in to it. You are stronger than you give yourself credit for. Fight daily against the temptations of the enemy, ask God for help and remember that there is always an escape route waiting for you, so don't take the bait.

NOTES:

December 7
Power To Destroy Strongholds

2 Corinthians 10:3-4 (ESV)

God has given you power to destroy strongholds. You do not wage war against the flesh although you walk in flesh, but you wage war in the spirit. God has given you the power to destroy strongholds in the spiritual realm. Every attack that comes at you is in the spirit, although at times it seems as if it's in the flesh. The power that has been given to you from God can break every chain in your life, it can break every addiction, it can break every soul tie and it can break every generational curse. There is a battle going on and you have to be willing to fight for your life.

NOTES:

December 8
The Finish Line Awaits You

1 Timothy 6:12 (ESV)

You have been given one life, so live it according to God's will. Walk in faith knowing that God knows the end, at the beginning. For what awaits you in eternity, is what God has called you to when you professed Jesus Christ as your Lord and Savior. Live life as if you're running a race and get to the finish line, no matter what it takes. You are equipped for everything that God sends your way, as he would never put on you more than you can bear. You have to fight for what you want out of life, for nothing worth having comes easy. You've been given this life because only you could endure it. Keep striving for greatness.

NOTES:

December 9
A Willing Heart Of Obedience

Titus 2:11-12 (ESV)

You've been born into the world but you are not of the world. God has called you to live a self-controlled, upright and Godly lifestyle. This is often something hard to do, yet if it were impossible God would have not given us the task. No matter what has taken place in your life, what is currently taking place and what will take place in the future, you are an example of Christ to someone on the earth. You will lead someone to salvation. You don't have to have it all together, but you do need to have a willing heart to obey God. God has used so many individuals who were not qualified by the world's standards, but were qualified by God's standards to win souls for his kingdom. God can use anyone, at any moment, to make sure that his will is being done on earth. Do not disqualify yourself, because God has qualified you.

NOTES:

December 10
Be Steadfast And Disciplined

1 Peter 4:7 (NIV)

The end of the world is coming soon, although no man knows the day nor the hour. Continue to be steadfast and disciplined in your prayers. As long as your heart is in the right place and you have forgiven those who you are holding a grudge against, your prayers will be heard. Learn not to only pray for yourself but pray for others also. For we don't know what tomorrow may bring, but we do know that when we ask God, things get accomplished; when we seek, we find what God wants to reveal to us, and when we knock, doors shall be opened for us. Make spending time with God something that you can't go a day without.

NOTES:

December 11
Obey God's Commands

Deuteronomy 28:13 (NIV)

There is only greatness that can come from your obedience to God. Remember that God is the creator of all things and he will never steer you in the wrong direction. If he has commanded you to do anything, it's for your benefit. When you obey the commands of God, he promises to make you the head and not the tail, above and not beneath, the lender and not the borrower. Learn to make wise choices with the decisions you make on a daily basis. God will reward those who earnestly seek after him and obey his Word. Obedience is better than sacrifice.

NOTES:

December 12
Power And Authority Over The Enemy

Luke 10:19 (ESV)

God has given you the power and authority to overcome the enemy. No matter which direction the enemy comes at you, you have the power to overcome him and his tactics. Keep in mind that Satan's whole objective is to kill, steal and destroy you by any means necessary. The enemy will never stop coming at you as long as you are here on this earth. Learn his tactics and use the authority that has been given to you to overcome every trap, scheme and ploy that he sets in place for you. You are more than a conqueror. Every day is a battle and every day your focus should be on overcoming the enemy in the battle, by using the power given to you by God. Stay on your guard at all times.

NOTES:

December 13
Win Souls

John 20:21-22 (ESV)

You have been chosen by God, to do a new work within his kingdom. You were born to be a disciple of Jesus Christ and win souls for the Kingdom of God. You've been given your own unique way of getting others interested in building a relationship with God. In doing what God has called you to do, he will give you peace through the process. There are many individuals following you, and for some you are the only Bible that people are reading. Make sure that you are being the best example of God on, the earth that you can be. Grow spiritually daily, be obedient to the Word of God, share your testimony, stay in the Word of God and continue to build an authentic relationship with Christ. You are called to be light in this world full of darkness.

NOTES:

December 14
Live The Word Of God

Revelation 2:26-27 (NLT)

It's important, not only to read the Word of God, but also to actually live the Word of God. When you are obedient in what God has called you to do there is no limit to where God will take you. Learn not to live for yourself or others, but to live for God all the days of your life. Allow the Holy Spirit to lead and guide you in the ways that you should go, so that you don't depart from the Word of God. When you align your life with God's will you will see things be established in your life. Things may not be falling together because you are not being obedient to the Word of God. Stop doing things your way and start doing things God's way, so that you can experience life in abundance.

NOTES:

December 15
Freedom Is In The Blood

Ephesians 1:7-8 (ESV)

Walk in freedom today. Jesus Christ paid the price on the cross so that you could be free. You are free from hurt, free from pain, free from burdens, free from unforgiveness, free from the curses that have been spoken over your life, free from what individuals have done to you, free from thinking that you're not good enough, free from having a negative mindset, free from low self-esteem, free from bondage of anything holding you back right now. Your freedom was purchased with the price of the blood of Jesus, which still covers you this day. Walk proudly with your head held high, knowing that you're no longer in bondage. You have to choose to walk in freedom today, because you are already free.

NOTES:

December 16
You Are Not Defeated

Hebrews 2:14 (ESV)

The power of the enemy was destroyed the moment Jesus Christ decided to die for you on the cross. Not only did Jesus share in human nature so that we would have an example of how to love God and love people, we also see how Jesus overcame the enemy with his blood, power and authority given to him by God. Never forget how much power and authority you hold against the enemy because Jesus died on the cross for you. There should never be a day that goes by where you feel defeated. Walk in the power and the authority given to you, by God, to defeat the enemy. You shall be victorious.

NOTES:

December 17
A Lifestyle Pleasing To God

Psalm 119:130 (NIV)

The Word of God is the guide to living a lifestyle that is pleasing to God. When you understand what is being explained in the Word of God you will begin to walk in wisdom and gain understanding. The more you study and understand the Bible, the more you are prepared to deal with what life brings your way. If you feel unprepared for anything in life, pick up the Bible. In the Word of God you will find people that you can relate to, situations that are similar to what you go through, advice for what you're facing right now, clarity for things that you don't understand and encouragement to keep moving forward no matter what your circumstances look like. Stay in the Word of God and be encouraged.

NOTES:

December 18
The Bible Is Truth

Psalm 119:160 (NIV)

The Word of God will stand forever. If you want truth, read the Bible. Even if you aren't ready to face the truth about you or your situation, allow God to transform your heart. When you get the Word of God in your spirit you become accountable for what is poured into you. Don't be afraid of this. God wants to grow you up and show you ways to please him, regardless of what you've been through and regardless of what you've done in your past. We serve a God who holds no grudges and who keeps no record of wrong. You're missing out on the greatness that is God, when you aren't committed totally to your relationship with him and to his Word. Make a change today, surrender totally to God and watch your life change in miraculous ways.

NOTES:

December 19
God's Word Cannot Fail

Isaiah 46:10-11 (GNT)

There is nothing hidden from you by God. Everything that God has said to you in prayer and through his Word shall be accomplished. From the beginning it has been predicted what will happen, and all those things shall come to pass. If you believe God wholeheartedly, you should believe that what he has spoken to you in your time of solitude will come to pass. Don't be discouraged and don't be in such a hurry that you begin doing things in your own strength. What God has for you, is for you. The plan God has for you will be established. Your life has meaning, your purpose will be fulfilled and you shall walk into your destiny. I encourage you today to stand on the Word of God and the promises that he has made to you. God cannot fail.

NOTES:

December 20
Seek First The Kingdom Of God

Isaiah 55:11 (NLT)

The Word of God will not return to you void. Everything that comes from God is good and it will be established here on earth. The Word of God is sent out and it will always produce fruit. When you are obedient to the Word of God, everything that aligns with the will of God will prosper. When you submit all your plans to God, you will see them be established. Get out of the mind frame that things have to be done your way and on your timing. If what you want out of life aligns with God's will for your life, it will not pass you by. If things don't happen how you want them to and things aren't going as you planned, seek God and allow his will to be done in your life. Nothing happens in your life without the approval of God. Seek first the Kingdom of God and all things shall be added unto you.

NOTES:

December 21
You Are A Messenger To The World

Ezekiel 2:7 (NLT)

Think of yourself as God's messenger. When you read the Word, hide the Word in your heart and live the Word, you are well equipped to speak the Word of God. Everyone that you come in contact with will not listen or obey the Word of God. What God requires from you is to relay the message. There are so many individuals that we love and care for that will never accept the Word of God; this is not your problem. God has chosen you to be his messenger, as you are his disciple. You can't live life for others. You can only do what God has called you to do. Take nothing personal as God's messenger. His Word will saturate the hearts of those you come in contact with. Allow God to work in you and through you, as you carry the light of Christ everywhere you go.

NOTES:

December 22
Stand Firm On God's Promises

Ezekiel 12:28 (NLT)

Be thankful that what God says shall come to pass. Every word that he has spoken shall be performed. Miracles will take place. Prophecies will be established. Lives will be saved. Individuals will turn from their wicked ways. What Satan meant for evil, God shall turn it into good. Each day that you live and breathe you see God working in ways that only he can. Stand on the promises of the Word of God and bask in his glory all the days of your life.

NOTES:

December 23
The Road To Heaven Is Narrow

John 8:51 (ESV)

There is a promise that God has given to his children, about obedience to his Word. If you keep his Word, you will never see death. Everyone will see a natural death, but everyone will not see a spiritual death. If you are a child of God and you keep his promises, his promise to you is that you will live in eternity, with him, all the days of your life. What you do in this lifetime will determine where you spend eternity. For the road to heaven is narrow and only a few pass through. Remember that your life matters to God, so make it count.

NOTES:

December 24
The Impossible Made Possible

John 6:63 (ESV)

God is the plug. God's spirit is what gives you power. Human power is of no use without the spirit of God. If ever you are doing anything in your own strength, it will not work. God did not create you to be set apart from him. Everything and anything that you accomplish on this earth is through the strength and anointing of the Holy Spirit. You may take credit for it, but you didn't accomplish it. Yes, you may have put in work to fulfill it, but without God's life-giving spirit, you can't accomplish anything. Give glory to God today, knowing that with him, nothing is impossible.

NOTES:

December 25
Never Stop Believing

2 Timothy 2:9 (ESV)

A warning was sent to us through Jesus Christ that we would be persecuted for his sake. So don't be caught off guard when things that you've been warned about begin to take place. Through it all, God is with you and his Word will not return to you void. The enemy will come at you the hardest and use anyone he can, to get to you. Stand strong, steadfast and immovable in the Word of God and watch God's words be established. Never stop believing in the miraculous powers of what God can do. What God is doing in you and through you is a miracle in itself. Hide the Word of the Lord in your heart, so that it will never depart from you.

NOTES:

December 26
Praise Worthy

Psalm 150 (ESV)

God deserves your praise. Not only for what he has done or what he will do for you, but just for who he is. God is The Alpha and The Omega and he deserves your praise. God is ruler over everything and he deserves your praise. God can make all things possible and he deserves your praise. God has brought you from a mighty long way and he deserves your praise. God is always with you and he deserves your praise. God has qualified you and he deserves your praise. God has instilled greatness within you and he deserves your praise. God has given you many gifts and talents and you should use them to give him praise. Glorify God today and praise him like never before. There is nothing that we can do to ever repay God, but to offer up our praise.

NOTES:

December 27
Bless God In Advance

Ephesians 1:3 (NIV)

You are not deserving of everything that is showered upon you by God, yet he never stops reigning down blessings on his people. Your life is blessed, your family is blessed, your finances are blessed, your home is blessed and your business is blessed. You have to speak things into existence and bless God in advance for what is about to take place. Even when you don't see it with your natural eyes, God is always working behind the scenes on your behalf. When you praise God just for who he is, you'll see him move in miraculous ways on your behalf. Never stop giving glory to God.

NOTES:

December 28
Saturate Yourself In God's Love

Nehemiah 8:10 (NIV)

Rejoice and be glad, for today is the day that the Lord has made. Wake up each day knowing that it is a special day that was set apart for you, by God. God has called you to do something great in this day; don't take it for granted. You may not know what the outcome of today will bring, but be encouraged to keep your eyes focused on Jesus. Your peace comes from God. Your joy comes from God. Your light comes from God. Your positive attitude comes from God. Your favor comes from God. Allow God's love to saturate you today. Feel his presence and bask in it, for today is a day that you can't get back.

NOTES:

December 29
Stay Encouraged During The Process

James 5:8 (ESV)

Patience is a virtue. We would rather things take place right when we want them, instead of waiting for God to establish them. There is strength in patience, there is wisdom in patience, there is clarity in patience, there is understanding in patience and there is growth in patience. What God wants you to have will be given to you. Whether things take a day, a week, a month or a year to accomplish, God is in control of all things. Stay encouraged during the process and don't lose hope. Stay focused on what God wants you to accomplish instead of focusing on what you want to be accomplished. God has your best interest at heart and he holds the key to all things.

NOTES:

December 30
Never Give Up On God

Isaiah 65:24 (ESV)

God is an *on time* God and he always has your best interest at heart. While you are praying to him, he is answering your prayers. Don't ever give up on God, because he will never give up on you. God knows what you need, what you want and what you desire before you even speak it. Hold on, he's coming. God's blessings are on the way. You will never go without what you need, you will receive some of the things that you want, and when your desires align will God's will, you will see them accomplished. After you pray, begin to praise God, knowing that he has your best interest at heart and his plans for your life are more than you can imagine. Thank you, Lord, for answered prayers.

NOTES:

December 31
The Victory Is Yours

Deuteronomy 20:4, 28:7 (ESV)

Walk in victory today, knowing that anything that did not come from God will not prosper against you. You have the victory, learn to walk in it. God is your refuge and your shield. God is always with you, which guarantees you the victory. Walk in love and walk in light knowing that God will make your enemies your footstool. When God fights for you, you're guaranteed to win. The victory is yours, declares the Lord!

NOTES:

Made in the USA
Columbia, SC
18 June 2021

40600347R00211